Professional Examinations

Managerial Level

Subject F2

Advanced Financial Reporting

EXAM PRACTICE KIT

British Library Cataloguing-in-Publication Data

A catalogue record for this book is available from the British Library.

Published by:

Kaplan Publishing UK
Unit 2 The Business Centre
Molly Millar's Lane
Wokingham
Berkshire
RG41 2QZ

ISBN: 978-1-78740-212-6

© Kaplan Financial Limited, 2018

The text in this material and any others made available by any Kaplan Group company does not amount to advice on a particular matter and should not be taken as such. No reliance should be placed on the content as the basis for any investment or other decision or in connection with any advice given to third parties. Please consult your appropriate professional adviser as necessary. Kaplan Publishing Limited, all other Kaplan group companies, the International Accounting Standards Board, and the IFRS Foundation expressly disclaim all liability to any person in respect of any losses or other claims, whether direct, indirect, incidental, consequential or otherwise arising in relation to the use of such materials. Printed and bound in Great Britain.

Acknowledgements

This Product includes propriety content of the International Accounting Standards Board which is overseen by the IFRS Foundation, and is used with the express permission of the IFRS Foundation under licence. All rights reserved. No part of this publication may be reproduced, stored in a retrieval system, or transmitted in any form or by any means, electronic, mechanical, photocopying, recording, or otherwise, without prior written permission of Kaplan Publishing and the IFRS Foundation.

IFRS

The IFRS Foundation logo, the IASB logo, the IFRS for SMEs logo, the "Hexagon Device", "IFRS Foundation", "eIFRS", "IAS", "IASB", "IFRS for SMEs", "IFRS", "IASs", "IFRSs", "International Accounting Standards" and "International Financial Reporting Standards", "IFRIC" and "IFRS Taxonomy" are Trade Marks of the IFRS Foundation.

IFRS

Trade Marks

The IFRS Foundation logo, the IASB logo, the IFRS for SMEs logo, the "Hexagon Device", "IFRS Foundation", "eIFRS", "IAS", "IASB", "IFRS for SMEs", "NIIF" IASs" "IFRS", "IFRSs", "International Accounting Standards", "International Financial Reporting Standards", "IFRIC", "SIC" and "IFRS Taxonomy".

Further details of the Trade Marks including details of countries where the Trade Marks are registered or applied for are available from the Foundation on request.

This product contains material that is ©Financial Reporting Council Ltd (FRC). Adapted and reproduced with the kind permission of the Financial Reporting Council. All rights reserved. For further information, please visit www.frc.org.uk or call +44 (0)20 7492 2300.

Chartered Institute of
Management Accountants

How to access your on-line resources

Kaplan Financial students will have a MyKaplan account and these extra resources will be available to you online. You do not need to register again, as this process was completed when you enrolled. If you are having problems accessing online materials, please ask your course administrator.

If you are not studying with Kaplan and did not purchase your book via a Kaplan website, to unlock your extra online resources please go to www.en-gage.co.uk (even if you have set up an account and registered books previously). You will then need to enter the ISBN number (on the title page and back cover) and the unique pass key number contained in the scratch panel below to gain access.

You will also be required to enter additional information during this process to set up or confirm your account details.

If you purchased through Kaplan Flexible Learning or via the Kaplan Publishing website you will automatically receive an e-mail invitation to register your details and gain access to your content. If you do not receive the e-mail or book content, please contact Kaplan Publishing.

Your code and information

This code can only be used once for the registration of one book online. This registration and your online content will expire when the final sittings for the examinations covered by this book have taken place. Please allow one hour from the time you submit your book details for us to process your request.

Please scratch the film to access your unique code.

Please be aware that this code is case-sensitive and you will need to include the dashes within the passcode, but not when entering the ISBN.

CONTENTS

	Page
Index to questions and answers	P.5
Examination techniques	P.7
Syllabus guidance, learning objectives and verbs	P.9
Approach to revision	P.13

Section

1	Objective test questions	1
2	Answers to objective test questions	87
3	References	153

This document references IFRS® Standards and IAS® Standards, which are authored by the International Accounting Standards Board (the Board), and published in the 2016 IFRS Standards Red Book.

Quality and accuracy are of the utmost importance to us so if you spot an error in any of our products, please send an email to mykaplanreporting@kaplan.com with full details.

Our Quality Co-ordinator will work with our technical team to verify the error and take action to ensure it is corrected in future editions.

SUBJECT F2 : ADVANCED FINANCIAL REPORTING

INDEX TO QUESTIONS AND ANSWERS

OBJECTIVE TEST QUESTIONS

	Page number	
	Question	*Answer*
Sources of finance (Questions 1 to 30)	**1**	**87**
– Long term finance	1	87
– Cost of capital and yield to maturity	3	88
Financial reporting (I) (Questions 31 to 88)	**6**	**90**
International accounting standards		
– IAS 32 & IFRS 9 *Financial instruments*	6	90
– IFRS 2 *Share based payments*	12	96
– IAS 33 *Earnings per share*	14	97
– IFRS 16 *Leases*	16	99
– IFRS 15 *Revenue from contracts with customers*	18	100
– IAS 37 *Provisions, contingent liabilities and contingent assets*	22	103
– IAS 12 *Taxation*	23	104
– IAS 24 *Related parties*	24	105
Financial reporting (II) (Questions 89 to 152)	**25**	**105**
Consolidated financial statements		
– Basic groups	25	105
– Complex groups (indirect holdings)	32	113
– Changes in groups structure	35	116
– Consolidated cash flow statements	41	120
– Foreign currency consolidations	44	122
Analysis of financial performance and position (Questions 153 to 202)	**48**	**124**
Random question tests	**69**	**135**
– Test 1	69	135
– Test 2	72	138
– Test 3	76	142
– Test 4	79	145
– Test 5	83	148

SUBJECT F2 : ADVANCED FINANCIAL REPORTING

EXAM TECHNIQUES

COMPUTER-BASED ASSESSMENT

TEN GOLDEN RULES

1. Make sure you have completed the compulsory 15 minute tutorial before you start exam. This tutorial is available through the CIMA website. You cannot speak to the invigilator once you have started.

2. These exam practice kits give you plenty of exam style questions to practise so make sure you use them to fully prepare.

3. Attempt all questions, there is no negative marking.

4. Double check your answer before you put in the final answer although you can change your response as many times as you like.

5. Not all questions will be multi choice questions (MCQs) – you may have to fill in missing words or figures.

6. Identify the easy questions first and get some points on the board to build up your confidence.

7. Try and allow 15 minutes at the end to check your answers and make any corrections.

8. Attempt "wordy" questions first as these may be quicker than the computation style questions. This will relieve some of the time pressure you will be under during the exam.

9. If you don't know the answer, flag the question and attempt it later. In your final review before the end of the exam try a process of elimination.

10. Work out your answer on the whiteboard provided first if it is easier for you. There is also an onscreen 'scratch pad' on which you can make notes. You are not allowed to take pens, pencils, rulers, pencil cases, phones, paper or notes.

SUBJECT F2 : ADVANCED FINANCIAL REPORTING

SYLLABUS GUIDANCE, LEARNING OBJECTIVES AND VERBS

A AIMS OF THE SYLLABUS

The aims of the syllabus are

- to provide for the Institute, together with the practical experience requirements, an adequate basis for assuring society that those admitted to membership are competent to act as management accountants for entities, whether in manufacturing, commercial or service organisations, in the public or private sectors of the economy

- to enable the Institute to examine whether prospective members have an adequate knowledge, understanding and mastery of the stated body of knowledge and skills

- to complement the Institute's practical experience and skills development requirements.

B STUDY WEIGHTINGS

A percentage weighting is shown against each topic in the syllabus. This is intended as a guide to the proportion of study time each topic requires.

All component learning outcomes will be tested and one question may cover more than one component learning outcome.

The weightings do not specify the number of marks that will be allocated to topics in the examination.

C LEARNING OUTCOMES

Each topic within the syllabus contains a list of learning outcomes, which should be read in conjunction with the knowledge content for the syllabus. A learning outcome has two main purposes:

1. to define the skill or ability that a well-prepared candidate should be able to exhibit in the examination

2. to demonstrate the approach likely to be taken by examiners in examination questions.

The learning outcomes are part of a hierarchy of learning objectives. The verbs used at the beginning of each learning outcome relate to a specific learning objective, e.g. Evaluate alternative approaches to budgeting.

The verb 'evaluate' indicates a high-level learning objective. As learning objectives are hierarchical, it is expected that at this level students will have knowledge of different budgeting systems and methodologies and be able to apply them.

A list of the learning objectives and the verbs that appear in the syllabus learning outcomes and examinations follows and these will help you to understand the depth and breadth required for a topic and the skill level the topic relates to.

SUBJECT F2 : ADVANCED FINANCIAL REPORTING

Learning objectives	Verbs used	Definition
1 Knowledge		
What you are expected to know	List	Make a list of
	State	Express, fully or clearly, the details of/facts of
	Define	Give the exact meaning of
2 Comprehension		
What you are expected to understand	Describe	Communicate the key features of
	Distinguish	Highlight the differences between
	Explain	Make clear or intelligible/State the meaning of
	Identify	Recognise, establish or select after consideration
	Illustrate	Use an example to describe or explain something
3 Application		
How you are expected to apply your knowledge	Apply	To put to practical use
	Calculate/compute	To ascertain or reckon mathematically
	Demonstrate	To prove with certainty or to exhibit by practical means
	Prepare	To make or get ready for use
	Reconcile	To make or prove consistent/compatible
	Solve	Find an answer to
	Tabulate	Arrange in a table
4 Analysis		
How you are expected to analyse the detail of what you have learned	Analyse	Examine in detail the structure of
	Categorise	Place into a defined class or division
	Compare and contrast	Show the similarities and/or differences between
	Construct	To build up or compile
	Discuss	To examine in detail by argument
	Interpret	To translate into intelligible or familiar terms
	Produce	To create or bring into existence
5 Evaluation		
How you are expected to use your learning to evaluate, make decisions or recommendations	Advise	To counsel, inform or notify
	Evaluate	To appraise or assess the value of
	Recommend	To advise on a course of action
	Advise	To counsel, inform or notify

D OBJECTIVE TEST

The most common types of Objective Test questions are:

- multiple choice, where you have to choose the correct answer(s) from a list of possible answers. This could either be numbers or text.

- multiple choice with more choices and answers – for example, choosing two correct answers from a list of eight possible answers. This could either be numbers or text.

- single numeric entry, where you give your numeric answer e.g. profit is $10,000.

- multiple entry, where you give several numeric answers e.g. the charge for electricity is $2000 and the accrual is $200.

- true/false questions, where you state whether a statement is true or false e.g. external auditors report to the directors is FALSE.

- matching pairs of text e.g. the convention 'prudence' would be matched with the statement' inventories revalued at the lower of cost and net realisable value'.

- other types could be matching text with graphs and labelling graphs/diagrams.

In this Exam Practice Kit we have used these types of questions.

Some further guidance from CIMA on number entry questions is as follows:

- For number entry questions, you do not need to include currency symbols or other characters or symbols such as the percentage sign, as these will have been completed for you. You may use the decimal point but must not use any other characters when entering an answer (except numbers) so, for example, $10,500.80 would be input as 10500.80.

- When expressing a decimal, for example a probability or correlation coefficient, you should include the leading zero (i.e. you should input 0.5 not .5).

- Negative numbers should be input using the minus sign, for example –1000.

- You will receive an error message if you try to enter a character or symbol that is not permitted (for example a '£' or '%' sign).

- A small range of answers will normally be accepted, taking into account sensible rounding.

SUBJECT F2 : ADVANCED FINANCIAL REPORTING

Guidance re CIMA On-Screen calculator:

As part of the computer based assessment software, candidates are now provided with a calculator. This calculator is on-screen and is available for the duration of the assessment. The calculator is accessed by clicking the calculator button in the top left hand corner of the screen at any time during the assessment.

All candidates must complete a 15 minute tutorial before the assessment begins and will have the opportunity to familiarise themselves with the calculator and practise using it.

Candidates may practise using the calculator by downloading and installing the practice exam at http://www.vue.com/athena/. The calculator can be accessed from the fourth sample question (of 12).

Please note that the practice exam and tutorial provided by Pearson VUE at http://www.vue.com/athena/ is not specific to CIMA and includes the full range of question types the Pearson VUE software supports, some of which CIMA does not currently use.

The Objective Tests are ninety minute computer-based assessments comprising 60 compulsory questions, with one or more parts. CIMA is continuously developing the question styles within the system and you are advised to try the online website demo at www.cimaglobal.com, to both gain familiarity with assessment software and examine the latest style of questions being used.

APPROACH TO REVISION

Stage 1: Assess areas of strengths and weaknesses

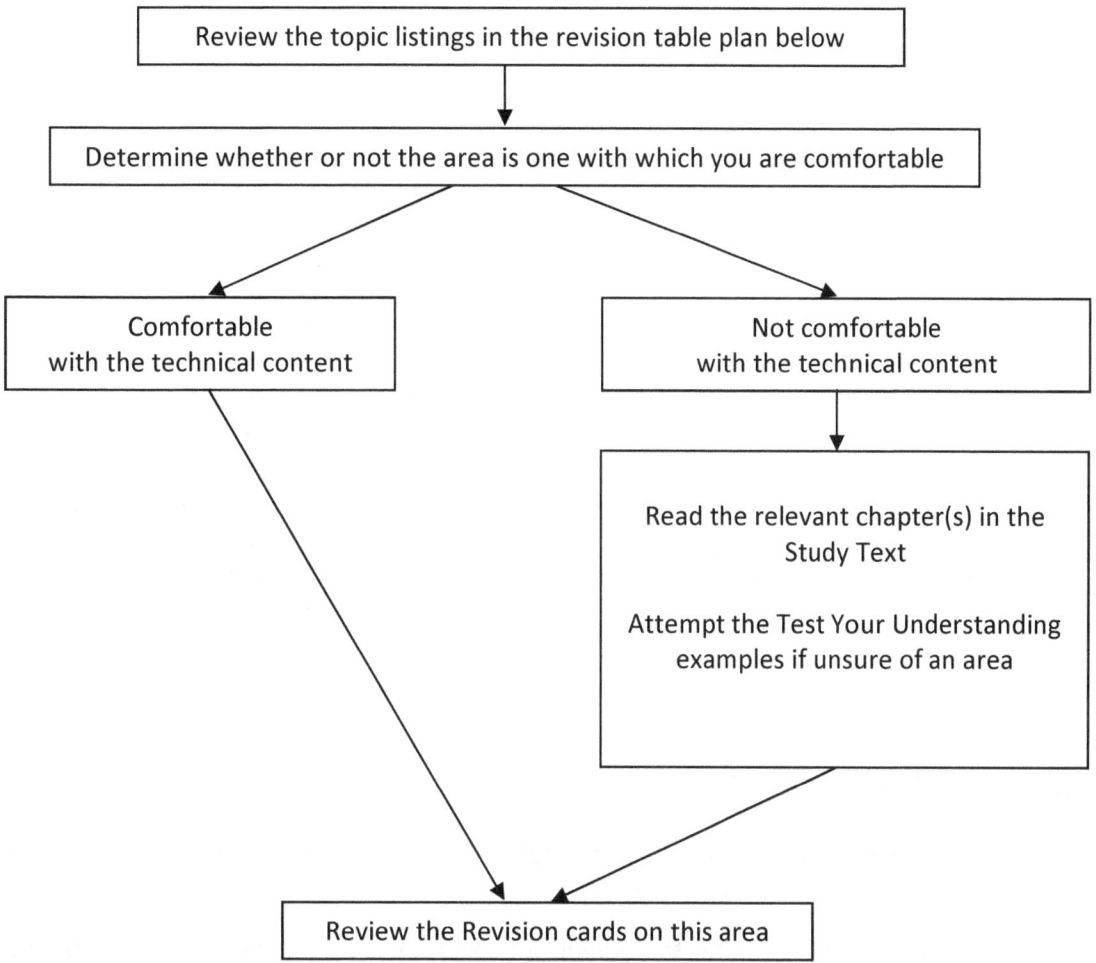

SUBJECT F2 : ADVANCED FINANCIAL REPORTING

Stage 2: Question practice

Follow the order of revision of topics as recommended in the revision table plan below and attempt the questions in the order suggested.

Try to avoid referring to text books and notes and the model answer until you have completed your attempt.

Try to answer the question in the allotted time.

Review your attempt with the model answer and assess how much of the answer you achieved in the allocated exam time.

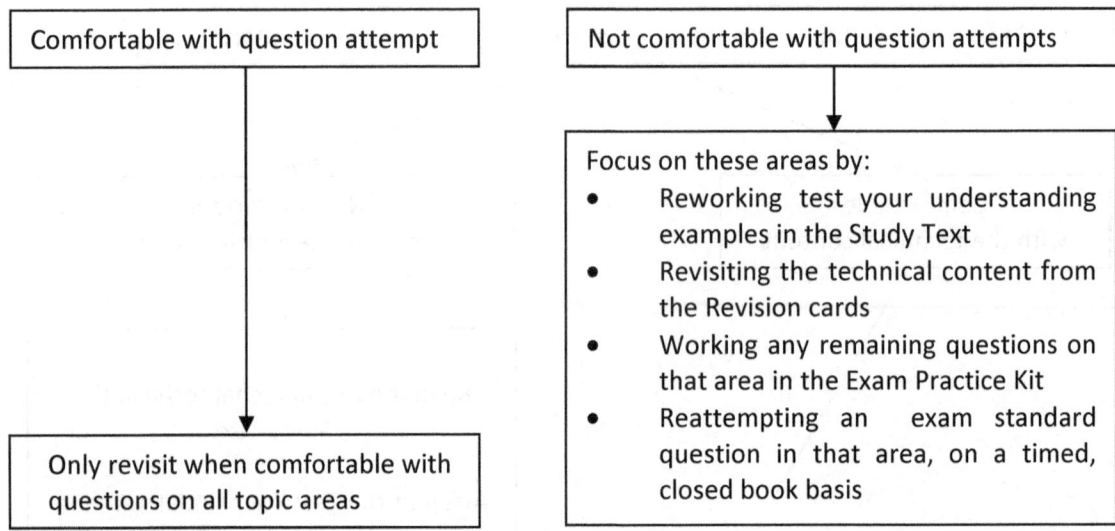

Stage 3: Final pre-exam revision

We recommend that you **attempt at least one ninety minute mock examination** containing a set of previously unseen exam standard questions.

It is important that you get a feel for the breadth of coverage of a real exam without advanced knowledge of the topic areas covered – just as you will expect to see on the real exam day.

Ideally a mock examination offered by your tuition provider should be sat in timed, closed book, real exam conditions.

F2
ADVANCED FINANCIAL REPORTING

Syllabus overview

F2 builds on the competencies gained from F1. It covers how to effectively source the long-term finance required to fund the operations of organisations, particularly their capital investments. It also deepens the coverage of financial reporting to more complex aspects of group accounting and analyses the rules governing the recognition and measurement of various elements of the financial statements. Finally it shows how to analyse financial statements to provide insights about the financial performance and position of the organisation over time and in comparison with others.

Summary of syllabus

Weight	Syllabus topic
15%	A. Sources of long-term finance
60%	B. Financial reporting
25%	C. Analysis of financial performance and position

SUBJECT F2 : ADVANCED FINANCIAL REPORTING

F2 – A. SOURCES OF LONG-TERM FINANCE (15%)

Learning outcomes
On completion of their studies, students should be able to:

Lead	Component	Indicative syllabus content
1 **discuss types and sources of long-term finance for an incorporated entity.**	(a) discuss the characteristics of different types of long-term debt and equity finance	• Characteristics of ordinary and preference shares and different types of long-term debt.
	(b) discuss the markets for and methods of raising long-term finance.	• Operation of the stock and bond markets. • Share and bond issues. • Role of advisors.
2 **calculate a weighted average cost of capital (WACC) for an incorporated entity.**	(a) calculate the cost of equity for an incorporated entity using the dividend valuation model	• Cost of equity using the dividend valuation model, with and without growth in dividends.
	(b) calculate the post-tax cost of debt for an incorporated entity	• Post-tax cost of bank borrowings. • Yield to maturity of bonds and post-tax cost of bonds. • Post-tax cost of convertible bonds up to and including conversion.
	(c) calculate the weighted average cost of capital (WACC) for an incorporated entity.	• WACC and its use.

F2 – B. FINANCIAL REPORTING (60%)

Learning outcomes
On completion of their studies, students should be able to:

Lead	Component	Indicative syllabus content

1 produce consolidated primary financial statements, incorporating accounting transactions and adjustments, in accordance with relevant international accounting standards, in an ethical manner.	(a) produce primary financial statements for a group of entities in accordance with relevant international accounting standards	• Production of:
		  – consolidated statement of comprehensive income
		  – consolidated statement of financial position
		  – consolidated statement of changes in equity
		  – consolidated statement of cash flows including the adoption of both full consolidation and the principles of equity accounting, in accordance with the provisions of IAS 1, IAS 27, IAS 28, IFRS 3, IFRS 10 and IFRS 11.

	(b) discuss the need for and nature of disclosure of interests in other entities	• The need for and nature of disclosure of interests in other entities, in accordance with IFRS 12.

	(c) discuss the provisions of relevant international accounting standards in respect of the recognition and measurement of revenue, leases, financial instruments, provisions, share-based payments and deferred taxation	• The need for and nature of disclosures of contingent assets and liabilities, in accordance with IAS 37.
		• Recognition and measurement of:
		  – revenue, in accordance with IAS 18 and the provisions of the framework
		  – operating and finance leases, in accordance with IAS 17
		  – financial instruments, excluding hedge accounting, in accordance with IAS 32 and IFRS 9 (or IAS 39 before effective date of IFRS 9)
		  – provisions, in accordance with IAS 37
		  – share-based payments, in accordance with IFRS 2
		  – provision for deferred taxation, in accordance with IAS 12.
		  – construction contracts in accordance with IAS 11.

	(d) produce the accounting entries, in accordance with relevant international accounting standards	
	(e) discuss the ethical selection and adoption of relevant accounting policies and accounting estimates.	• Ethics in financial reporting.

SUBJECT F2 : ADVANCED FINANCIAL REPORTING

Learning outcomes
On completion of their studies, students should be able to:

Lead	Component	Indicative syllabus content
2 **demonstrate the impact on the preparation of the consolidated financial statements of certain complex group scenarios.**	(a) demonstrate the impact on the group financial statements of: i acquiring additional shareholdings in the period ii disposing of all or part of a shareholding in the period	• Additional acquisition in the period resulting in a simple investment becoming a controlling interest, in accordance with the provisions of IFRS 3. • Calculation of the gain/loss on the disposal of a controlling interest in a subsidiary in the year, in accordance with the provisions of IFRS 3. • Adjustment to parent's equity resulting from acquiring or disposing of shares in a subsidiary, in accordance with the provisions of IFRS 3.
	(b) demonstrate the impact on the group financial statements of consolidating a foreign subsidiary	• Provisions of IAS 21 in respect of consolidating a foreign subsidiary and the calculation of the foreign exchange gains and losses in the period.
	(c) demonstrate the impact on the group financial statements of acquiring indirect control of a subsidiary.	• Impact of indirect effective holdings on the preparation of group financial statements.
3 **discuss the need for and nature of disclosure of transactions between related parties.**	(a) discuss the need for and nature of disclosure of transactions between related parties	• The need for and nature of disclosure of related party transactions, in accordance with IAS 24.
4 **produce the disclosures for earnings per share.**	(a) produce the disclosures for earnings per share.	• Calculate basic and diluted earnings per share, in accordance with IAS 33.

F2 – C. ANALYSIS OF FINANCIAL PERFORMANCE AND POSITION (25%)

Learning outcomes
On completion of their studies, students should be able to:

Lead	Component	Indicative syllabus content
1 evaluate the financial performance, financial position and financial adaptability of an incorporated entity.	(a) calculate ratios relevant for the assessment of an entity's profitability, financial performance, financial position and financial adaptability	• Ratios for profitability, performance, efficiency, activity, liquidity and gearing.
	(b) evaluate the financial performance, financial position and financial adaptability of an entity based on the information contained in the financial statements provided	• Interpretation of the primary financial statements and any additional information provided.
	(c) advise on action that could be taken to improve an entity's financial performance and financial position.	• Action that could be realistically taken by the entity's management to improve financial performance and strengthen financial position, taking into account ethical considerations and internal and external constraints.
2 discuss the limitations of ratio analysis.	(a) discuss the limitations of ratio analysis based on financial statements that can be caused by internal and external factors.	• Inter-segment comparisons. • International comparisons.

TABLES AND FORMULAE

'Information concerning formulae and tables will be provided via the CIMA website, www.cimaglobal.com, and your EN-gage login.'

Section 1

OBJECTIVE TEST QUESTIONS

SOURCES OF FINANCE

LONG TERM FINANCE

1   Which TWO of the following statements are true?
    A   Entities must be listed on a recognised stock exchange in order to be able to raise finance from the capital markets
    B   Only equity shares can be traded in the capital markets
    C   Bond holders are lenders of debt finance regardless of being traded on the capital markets
    D   If an entity is not listed on a stock market it cannot issue new shares
    E   The primary function of a stock market is to enable investors to buy and sell investments

2   Complete the sentences below by placing one of the following options in each of the spaces.

general assets	preferable
a specific asset	less preferable

    A floating charge is when debt is secured against _____ of the entity and this type of charge is considered _____ from the lenders point of view to a fixed charge.

3   Which one of the following statements is true in respect of raising equity finance?
    A   A rights issue is cheaper than a public share issue
    B   If an entity raises equity finance by way of a rights issue this would result in a flotation
    C   A rights issue will result in a dilution to existing shareholders' percentage ownership in the entity
    D   A rights issue is when equity shares are available to be purchased by institutional investors only

4   DF has raised finance via a rights issue of 1 for 5 at $2.25 per share. The shares were quoted at $2.75 prior to the rights issue.
    The theoretical ex rights price is:
    A $2.33
    B $2.50
    C $2.65
    D $2.67

5 Complete the sentences below by placing one of the following options in each of the spaces.

cum rights	ex rights

When a rights issue is announced, the existing shares will be traded _____ up to the date of the issue. After the issue takes place, the shares will then be traded _____.

6 Which one of the following statements is NOT a characteristic of cumulative preference shares?

A   Preference dividends must be paid before ordinary dividends can be paid

B   The entity cannot claim tax relief on preference dividends paid

C   If a dividend is not paid, it must be paid in a future period together with the normal dividend for that year

D   The directors can choose whether to pay the preference dividend or whether to delay it until a future period

7 Which TWO of the following statements are NOT characteristics of ordinary shares?

A   Dividends are paid at the discretion of the directors

B   Dividends are treated as a distribution of earnings and are paid out of post-tax profits

C   On the winding up of the entity, the shareholders will receive a payout before other types of shareholder

D   The dividend payment will be a fixed proportion of the nominal value of the shares

E   The shareholders have voting rights

8 ZX has made a rights issue of 1 for 3 at $6.75 per share. The shares were quoted at $7.50 prior to the rights issue.

Calculate the theoretical ex rights price. State your answer in $ to two decimal places.

9 Which one of the following statements is NOT an advantage of convertible debt?

A   The investor benefits from having the choice of redemption method

B   It may reduce the cash burden for the issuing entity at the redemption date

C   It allows the entity to offer lower coupon rates than would normally be required for debt instruments

D   The entity will not have to recognise a liability on the statement of financial position

10 Complete the sentences below by placing one of the following options in each of the spaces.

certainty	debt	equity	less	more	uncertainty

The providers of equity finance face _____ risk than the providers of debt finance because there is greater _____ over the level of their return. As a result _____ providers will require a higher level of return on their investment than _____ providers.

OBJECTIVE TEST QUESTIONS : **SECTION 1**

COST OF CAPITAL AND YIELD TO MATURITY

11 The ordinary shares of DS are quoted at $7.50 per share. A dividend of $0.60 per share is about to be paid. There is no growth in dividends expected.

Calculate the cost of equity using the dividend valuation model. State your answer as a percentage to one decimal place.

12 ED has just paid a dividend of 10 cents per share. ED's cost of equity (ke) is 15% and dividends are expected to grow by 3% per annum.

The ex-div share price of ED is (to the nearest cent):

A   67 cents

B   69 cents

C   83 cents

D   86 cents

13 **Complete the sentence below by placing one of the following options in the space.**

| cum div market price | ex div market price | nominal value |

When calculating the cost of preference shares, the dividend is divided by the _____ of the preference share.

14 JK plc, a listed entity, has in issue 10,000 6% coupon $100 nominal value irredeemable bonds. The current market value of each bond is $94.50.

Calculate the yield to maturity of the bonds. Give your answer as a percentage to 1 decimal place.

15 The equity shares of MC are quoted at $1.86 cum div with a dividend of 10 cents per share due to be paid.

Assuming that the growth rate in dividends is 3% a year, what is the cost of equity using the dividend model? Give your answer as a percentage to 1 decimal place.

16 ZX has in issue 5% convertible bonds with $100 nominal value each. Each bond is either redeemable at a premium of 2% or convertible into 15 ordinary shares in five years' time. The current share price is $6 and this price is expected to grow at 4% per annum for the next five years.

Calculate the value that should be used as the redemption amount in the internal rate of return calculation, for assessing the cost of a bond.

Give your answer in $ to two decimal places.

17 RS has in issue 5% irredeemable debentures currently quoted at $88 per $100 nominal value.

RS pays corporate income tax at a rate of 20%.

The post-tax cost of debt of these irredeemable debentures to one decimal place is:

A   4.0%

B   4.5%

C   4.8%

D   5.7%

SUBJECT F2 : ADVANCED FINANCIAL REPORTING

18 Which one of the following statements is INCORRECT in respect of the cost of debt?

    A   The cost of debt of redeemable bonds is the internal rate of return of the relevant cash flows

    B   When calculating the cost of debt of redeemable bonds, the relevant cash outflows are the gross annual interest payments and the redemption value of the bonds

    C   When calculating the cost of convertible debt, an assumption is made that the debt holders will choose the higher of the cash and conversion option at the date of redemption

    D   When redeemable bonds are traded at par, the formula for irredeemable bonds can be used to calculate the cost of debt

19 OLP plc, a listed entity, has in issue 30,000 7% coupon $100 nominal value irredeemable bonds. The current market value of each bond is $92.75.

Calculate the yield to maturity of the bonds. Give your answer as a percentage to 1 decimal place.

20 The cost of equity of MB is 12.5% and the shares are currently quoted at $6.50. A dividend has recently been paid and the expected growth in dividends is 4%.

The dividend per share that was paid out (to the nearest cent) is:

    A   53 cents

    B   55 cents

    C   57 cents

    D   81 cents

21 WD has a cost of equity of 10%. It has just paid a dividend of $0.13 per share and its dividends are expected to grow at 5% per annum.

Calculate WD's current share price using the dividend model. Give your answer in $ to two decimal places.

22 GG has the following debt:

Debt:	$120 million of long dated bonds issued at par and paying a coupon rate of 6%. The debt is currently trading at $102 per $100 nominal.

The corporate income tax rate is 30%.

Calculate the post tax cost of debt for GG. Give your answer as a percentage to one decimal place.

23 TC has in issue 100,000 $100 par value convertible bonds. The bonds are either redeemable at a premium of 15% or convertible into 10 ordinary shares in five years' time. The current share price is $10.22 and dividends are expected to grow at 2% per annum.

When calculating the cost of the bonds, what value should be included in the internal rate of return calculation per bond at the redemption date?

    A $100.00

    B $102.20

    C $112.84

    D $115.00

OBJECTIVE TEST QUESTIONS : SECTION 1

24   WW's cost of equity is 15% and the yield on its debt is 8%. Its debt to equity ratio is 1:3 based on book value and 1:4 based on market value. The corporate income tax rate is 25%.

Calculate WW's weighted average cost of capital (WACC).

Give your answer as a percentage to one decimal place.

25   TP has the following reported in its statement of financial position as at 31 August 20X3:

Equity and liabilities	$m
Ordinary shares ($1 each)	10
Retained reserves	37
5% long dated bonds	8

The current share price is $1.20 and TP has consistently paid a dividend of 14 cents per share, giving a cost of equity of 11.7%. The bonds are currently trading at $87.50 per $100 nominal value. The post-tax cost of debt of the bonds is 6%.

The weighted average cost of capital (WACC) to one decimal place is:

A   8.9%

B   9.2%

C   9.4%

D   9.6%

26   PM has the following reported in its statement of financial position as at 31 March 20X2:

Equity and liabilities	$m
Ordinary shares ($1 each)	10
Retained earnings	60
7% irredeemable debentures	20

The current share price is $3.80 cum div and PM has consistently paid a dividend of 50 cents per share. The debentures are trading at $96 ex int. PM is subject to corporate income tax at a rate of 30%.

Which of the following shows the correct cost of debt and cost of equity to use in the calculation of PM's WACC?

A   Cost of debt = 4.9%

     Cost of equity = 13.2%

B   Cost of debt = 5.1%

     Cost of equity = 13.2%

C   Cost of debt = 4.9%

     Cost of equity = 15.2%

D   Cost of debt = 5.1%

     Cost of equity = 15.2%

27   KC has in issue some long-dated bonds and has a post-tax cost of debt of 4.89%. The bonds are currently trading at $92 per $100 nominal.

KC pays corporate income tax at a rate of 25%.

Calculate the coupon rate of the long-dated bonds. Give your answer to the nearest whole percentage.

SUBJECT F2 : ADVANCED FINANCIAL REPORTING

28 JN plc has 1 million $0.50 par value shares in issue that are trading at $1.22. It has recently paid a dividend of $120,000. Dividends are expected to grow at 5% per annum.

The cost of equity of JN plc, calculated using the dividend model, is:

A 9.8%

B 10.3%

C 15.3%

D 16.5%

29 Which one of the following statements is considered to be a limitation of using the weighted average cost of capital (WACC)?

A   Entities typically fund projects/investments from an existing pool of funds rather than specifically allocating one source of finance to each project

B   If short-term finance is used to fund long term projects, it can also be included in the WACC calculation

C   Not all debt is quoted and sometimes book values are used as approximations instead

D   WACC can be used as discount rate in net present value and internal rate of return calculations

30 FG plc, a listed entity, has 5% coupon, $100 nominal value bond in issue. The bonds are redeemable at a premium of 12% in 4 years' time. The current market value of the bonds is $97.

The net present value of the bond price, the annual interest and final redemption value at a discount rate of 5% is $12.91 (positive). The net present value of the same amounts at a discount rate of 10% is $4.65 (negative).

Calculate the yield to maturity of the bonds. Give your answer as a percentage to one decimal place.

FINANCIAL REPORTING (I)

INTERNATIONAL ACCOUNTING STANDARDS

IAS® 32 & IFRS® 9 *FINANCIAL INSTRUMENTS*

31 Complete the sentences below by placing one of the following options in each of the spaces.

asset	equity	interest	favourable
debt	liability	obligation	unfavourable

A financial instrument is any contract that gives rise to a financial _____ of one entity and a financial liability or _____ instrument of another entity.

A financial liability is any liability that is a contractual _____ to deliver cash or another financial asset to another entity or to exchange financial assets or liabilities under _____ conditions.

OBJECTIVE TEST QUESTIONS : SECTION 1

32 ROB issued 4 million $1 5% redeemable bonds on 1 January 20X1 at par. The associated costs of issue were $100,000 which were recorded as a finance cost in the statement of profit or loss. The bonds are redeemable at $4.5 million on 31 December 20X4 and the effective interest rate associated with them has been calculated at approximately 8.5%.

The interest on the bonds is payable annually in arrears and the amount due has been paid in the year to 31 December 20X1 and charged to finance costs in the statement of profit or loss. No other accounting entries have been recorded.

No other accounting entries have been recorded.

The journal entry required to correct the treatment of the bonds in the financial statements of ROB for the year ended 31 December 20X1 is:

A	Dr	Liability – bonds	$100,000	
	Cr	Finance costs	$100,000	
B	Dr	Finance costs	$31,500	
	Cr	Liability – bonds	$31,500	
C	Dr	Finance costs	$131,500	
	Cr	Liability – bonds	$131,500	
D	Dr	Finance costs	$140,000	
	Cr	Liability – bonds	$140,000	

33 LP issued $10 million 6% convertible bonds on 1 January 20X3 at their par value. The bonds are redeemable at par on 31 December 20X7 or can be converted at that date on the basis of two $1 equity shares for every $10 of nominal value of bonds held. The prevailing market interest rate for similar bonds without conversion rights is 8%.

The equity component recognised at initial recognition of the convertible bonds was correctly recorded at a value of $794,200.

Calculate the carrying amount of the liability component that would be reflected in LP's statement of financial position at 31 December 20X3.

Give your answer to the nearest $.

34 VB acquired 40,000 shares in another entity, JK, in March 20X2 for $2.68 per share. The investment was classified as fair value through comprehensive income (FVOCI) on initial recognition. The shares were trading at $2.96 per share on 31 July 20X2. Commission of 5% of the value of the transaction is payable on all purchases and disposals of shares.

Calculate the gain that would be credited to reserves in the year ended 31 July 20X2 in respect of the above financial instrument.

Give your answer to the nearest $.

35 AB issued a long-term debt instrument on 1 January 20X1 raising $3,400,000. The transaction costs associated with the issue were $200,000. The debt instrument has a nominal rate of interest payable of 6% and the interest is payable annually in arrears. The effective rate of interest on the instrument is approximately 7.05%.

The liability for this instrument at 31 December 20X1 will be calculated as follows:

Liability	$
Opening balance	
Plus: finance cost	
Less: interest paid	
Closing balance	X

Place ONE of the following options in each of the highlighted boxes in the above table:

3,200,000	3,400,000	3,600,000
204,000	225,600	239,700

36 TR often provides short term interest free loans to its employees. Loan repayments are deducted from the employee's subsequent salary until fully repaid.

In accordance with IFRS 9® *Financial Instruments* which one of the following would be a suitable classification for the loans?

- A Fair value through profit or loss financial asset
- B Amortised cost financial asset
- C Fair value through other comprehensive income financial asset
- D Amortised cost financial liability

37 On 1 January 20X2, AB issued 400,000 5% cumulative irredeemable preference shares at their nominal value of $1.00 each. The shares have been recorded within equity and the preference dividend is payable on 31 December 20X2.

Which one of the following statements is true?

- A It is correct to classify the shares as equity because they are irredeemable
- B Investors in AB's preferences shares face higher risk than if they invested in non-cumulative irredeemable preference shares
- C The issue will be recorded by debiting investments and crediting bank
- D The dividend payable should be included in AB's finance cost as a period expense

38 BG acquired a debt investment on 30 June 20X2 for $42,000 and classified the investment as FVOCI. At 31 December 20X2, the reporting date, BG recorded a gain of $18,000 in other components of equity in respect of the change in fair value of the investment.

BG then disposed of the debt investment on 31 July 20X3 for $65,000.

Calculate the total gain that would be recorded in the statement of profit or loss of BG in the year ended 31 December 20X3 in respect of the investment.

39 JH acquired 500,000 shares in X on 1 November 20X1 for $2.80 per share and classified this investment as held for trading. JH paid 0.5% commission on the value of the transaction to its broker. X's shares were trading at $3.42 on 31 December 20X1.

JH recorded the initial measurement of the shares correctly.

The journal entry required to record the subsequent measurement of the shares at 31 December 20X1 is:

	Account reference	$
Debit	Investment in shares	
Credit		

Place ONE of the following options in each of the boxes above:

Profit or loss	303,000
Reserves	310,000

40 GT entered into a forward contract on 31 October 20X2 to purchase 1,000 ounces of gold on 30 April 20X3 at a forward price of $1,200 per ounce. At 31 December 20X2, GT's reporting date, the forward price for purchasing gold was $1,280 per ounce.

The forward contract should appear in GT's statement of financial position at 31 December 20X2 as:

- A Financial asset of $80,000
- B Financial asset of $1,200,000
- C Financial liability of $1,200,000
- D Financial liability of $1,280,000

41 RF has entered into a factoring arrangement for a significant receivable balance of $9 million. It has received a cash advance from the factor of 85% of the value of the receivable and will receive the remaining 15% less an administrative fee when the customer settles the outstanding balance. If the factor does not recover the receivable balance within six months, it will recover the cash advance from RF and will charge the administrative fee.

Which one of the following statements is INCORRECT in respect of the above arrangement?

- A RF retains the significant risks and rewards of ownership of the receivables balance until the customer settles the amount
- B The administrative fee should be charged to the statement of profit or loss over the term of the factoring arrangement
- C An expense of $1,350,000 is initially recorded in the statement of profit or loss.
- D The cash advance should initially be recognised as a liability

42 EMS issued 5 million 6% redeemable $1 preference shares 20X8 at their nominal value on 1 January 20X2. The issue costs associated with the share issue were $200,000.

The journal entry required to initially recognise the preference shares in the financial statements of EMS at 1 January 20X2 is:

A	Dr	Bank	$4,800,000
	Cr	Equity	$4,800,000
B	Dr	Bank	$4,800,000
	Cr	Financial liability	$4,800,000
C	Dr	Bank	$4,800,000
	Dr	Profit or loss	$200,000
	Cr	Equity	$5,000,000
D	Dr	Bank	$4,800,000
	Dr	Profit or loss	$200,000
	Cr	Financial liability	$5,000,000

SUBJECT F2 : ADVANCED FINANCIAL REPORTING

43 MAT made an investment in a financial instrument on 1 January 20X2 at its nominal value of $2,000,000. The instrument carries a fixed coupon interest rate of 7% which is receivable annually in arrears. The instrument will be redeemed for $2,265,000 on 31 December 20X5. The business model of MAT is to intend to hold debt financial assets until maturity. Transaction costs of $100,000 were paid on acquisition.

The journal entry that initially records the instrument is:

A	Dr	Investment	$1,900,000
	Cr	Bank	$1,900,000
B	Dr	Investment	$2,000,000
	Dr	Statement of profit or loss	$100,000
	Cr	Bank	$2,100,000
C	Dr	Investment	$2,100,000
	Cr	Bank	$2,100,000
D	Dr	Investment	$1,900,000
	Dr	Statement of profit or loss	$100,000
	Cr	Bank	$2,000,000

44 BN issued $6 million 7% convertible bonds on 1 January 20X1 at par. The bonds are redeemable at par on 31 December 20X4 or convertible at that date on the basis of two $1 ordinary shares for every nominal $10 of bonds. At the date of issue the prevailing market rate of interest for similar debt without conversion rights was 9%.

The amount that should be credited to equity upon the initial recognition of convertible bonds on 1 January 20X1 is:

A $2,400
B $391,200
C $4,320,000
D $4,639,200

45 BCL entered into a forward contract on 31 July 20X0 to purchase B$2 million at a contracted rate of A$1: B$0.64 on 31 October 20X0. The contract cost was A$nil. BCL prepares its financial statements to 31 August 20X0. At 31 August 20X0 an equivalent contract for the purchase of B$2 million could be acquired at a rate of A$1: B$0.70

The journal entry that records this instrument in the financial statements for the year ended 31 August 20X0 is:

A	Dr	Derivative asset	A$ 120,000
	Cr	Profit or loss	A$ 120,000
B	Dr	Profit or loss	A$ 120,000
	Cr	Derivative liability	A$ 120,000
C	Dr	Derivative asset	A$ 267,857
	Cr	Profit or loss	A$ 267,857
D	Dr	Profit or loss	A$ 267,857
	Cr	Derivative liability	A$ 267,857

46 EMR made an investment in a debt instrument on 1 July 20X0 at its nominal value of $4,000,000. The instrument carries a fixed coupon interest rate of 7%, which is receivable annually in arrears. The instrument will be redeemed for $4,530,000 on 30 June 20X4. Transaction costs associated with the investment were $200,000 and were paid on 1 July 20X0. The effective interest rate applicable to this instrument has been calculated at approximately 8.4%. EMR's business model is to hold some debt financial assets until redemption but also to sell some of its debt financial assets.

The fair value of the debt instrument as at 30 June 20X1 is $4,500,000.

The impact of the investment in the statement of profit or loss and other comprehensive income for the year ended 30 June 20X1 is:

Statement of profit or loss extract	$
Profit from operations	X
Finance income	
Finance costs	
	———
Profit before tax	X
Other comprehensive income	
Gain on revaluation of FVOCI financial asset	

Place ONE of the following options in each of the highlighted boxes in the above table. Place 'BLANK' against the heading not required:

227,200	280,000
319,200	336,000
352,800	444,000
BLANK	

47 JK acquired 100% of the ordinary shares of OVS on 1 July 20X1 for $2,400,000. All of JK's investment transactions are conducted by a broker who charges 2% commission on the transaction value. JK has correctly classified and recorded its investment in OVS as a FVOCI asset. At 30 June 20X2 the investment in OVS has a fair value of $2,570,000.

The journal entry required in JK's individual financial statements to record the subsequent measurement of the investment at 30 June 20X2 is:

	Account reference	$
Debit	Investment in shares	
Credit		

Place ONE of the following options in each of the boxes above:

Profit or loss	122,000
Reserves	170,000

SUBJECT F2 : ADVANCED FINANCIAL REPORTING

48 CLW issued a $4 million 7% convertible bond on 1 January 20X2 at par value. The bond is redeemable at par on 31 December 20X6 or can be converted at that date on the basis of two $1 ordinary shares for every $10 of bonds held. The prevailing market interest rate for a similar bond without conversion rights was 9% per annum.

The journal entry required to initially record the convertible bond on 1 January 20X2 is:

	Account reference	$
Debit		4,000,000
Credit		
Credit	Equity	

Place ONE of the following options in each of the boxes above:

Bank	310,800
Financial asset	3,689,200
Financial liability	4,000,000
BLANK	

IFRS® 2 SHARE-BASED PAYMENTS

49 VB granted share options to its 500 employees on 1 August 20X0. Each employee will receive 1,000 share options they continue to work for VB for the four years following the grant date. The fair value of the options at the grant date was $1.30 each. In the year ended 31 July 20X1, 20 employees left and another 50 were expected to leave in the following three years. In the year ended 31 July 20X2, 18 employees left and a further 30 were expected to leave during the next two years.

Calculate the expense that would be recognised in VB's statement of profit or loss for the year ended 31 July 20X2 in respect of the share option, in accordance with IFRS 2 *Share-based Payments*.

Give your answer to the nearest $.

50 Complete the sentences below by placing one of the following options in each of the spaces.

cash-settled	equity	grant date
equity-settled	liabilities	reporting date

A share option scheme is an example of a/an _____ share-based payment, in which an expense should be recognised with an associated credit to _____ measured using the fair value at the _____.

A share appreciation rights scheme is an example of a/an _____ share-based payment, in which an expense should be recognised with an associated credit to _____ measured using the fair value at the _____.

51 RT granted 1,000 share appreciation rights (SARs) to each of its 500 employees on 1 July 20X0. To be eligible for the rights, employees must remain employed by RT for 3 years from the date of grant. The rights must be exercised in July 20X3, with settlement due in cash.

In the year to 30 June 20X1, 42 employees left and a further 75 were expected to leave over the following two years.

In the year to 30 June 20X2, 28 employees left and a further 25 were expected to leave in the following year.

The fair value of each SAR was $9 at 30 June 20X1 and $11 at 30 June 20X2.

The liability that would be recognised in the statement of financial position RT as at 30 June 20X2 in respect of the scheme is:

- A $1,149,000
- B $1,821,000
- C $2,430,000
- D $2,970,000

52 KOL granted share options to all of its 400 employees on 1 January 20X0. Each employee will receive 1,000 share options provided they continue to be employed by KOL for four years from the grant date. The fair value of an option was $2.20 at the grant date and $2.75 at 31 December 20X0.

At 1 January 20X0 it was estimated that 70 staff would leave over the next four years.

22 staff left in the first year of the scheme and at 31 December 20X0 the revised estimate of staff expected to leave over the next three years was 56.

The expense that would be recognised in the financial statements of KOL in the year ended 31 December 20X0 in respect of the scheme is:

- A $138,600
- B $177,100
- C $181,500
- D $221,375

53 KL granted 1,000 share appreciation rights (SARs) to its 120 employees on 1 December 20X7. To be eligible, employees must remain employed for 3 years from the grant date. The right must be exercised in December 20Y0.

In the year to 30 November 20X8, 12 staff left and a further 15 were expected to leave over the following two years. In the year to 30 November 20X9 8 staff left and a further 10 were expected to leave in the following year.

The fair value of each SAR was $15 at 30 November 20X8 and $17 at 30 November 20X9.

The journal entry required to record the charge to KL's profit or loss for the year ended 30 November 20X9 in respect of the SARs will be:

	Account reference	$
Debit	Profit or loss	
Credit		

Place ONE of the following options in each of the boxes above:

Non-current liabilities	465,000
Other components of equity	555,000
435,000	1,020,000

IAS® 33 EARNINGS PER SHARE

54 On 1 July 20X0 BNM, a listed entity, had 5 million $1 ordinary shares in issue. On 1 September 20X0, BNM made a 1 for 2 bonus issue from retained earnings. BNM generated profit after tax of $3.8 million for the year ended 30 June 20X1.

Calculate the basic earnings per share for the year ended 30 June 20X1.

Give your answer in cents to one decimal place.

55 On 1 October 20X1 VB, a listed entity, had 8 million $1 ordinary shares in issue. On 1 May 20X2 VB issued a further 2.4 million new $1 ordinary shares for $9.20, the full market price.

The consolidated profit for the year was $6,582,000 of which $420,000 was attributable to the non-controlling interest.

The consolidated basic earnings per share of VB for the year ended 30 September 20X2 is:

- A 67.0 cents per share
- B 68.5 cents per share
- C 73.1 cents per share
- D 77.8 cents per share

56 CB, a listed entity, had 3,000,000 ordinary shares in issue on 1 February 20X4. On 1 March 20X4, CB made a rights issue of 1 for 4 at $6.50 per share. The issue was fully taken up by the shareholders.

CB's share price immediately prior to the rights issue was $7.50, rising to $8.25 after the issue. The theoretical ex rights price relating to the rights issue is $7.30.

Calculate the weighted average number of shares that would be applied in the basic earnings per share calculation for the year ended 31 January 20X5.

Give your answer to the nearest whole number of shares.

57 The weighted average number of ordinary shares in issue for the year to 31 December 20X1 is 7 million and the profit for the year was $3.5 million resulting in basic earnings per share for the year of 50 cents.

Options to purchase 1,000,000 $1 ordinary shares at $3.10 per share were issued on 1 January 20X1. These options are exercisable between 1 January 20X2 and 31 December 20X4. The average market value of each $1 ordinary share during the year ended 31 December 20X1 is $4.00.

The diluted earnings per share, in cents to one decimal place, for the year ended 31 December 20X1 is:

- A 34.7 cents per share
- B 43.8 cents per share
- C 48.0 cents per share
- D 48.4 cents per share

58 Weighted average shares:
- 1 Jan – 31 Mar: 10,000,000 × 5/4 × 3/12 = 3,125,000
- 1 Apr – 31 Oct: 12,000,000 × 5/4 × 7/12 = 8,750,000
- 1 Nov – 31 Dec: 15,000,000 × 2/12 = 2,500,000
- Total weighted average = 14,375,000

Profit after tax = 14,375,000 × $0.06 = **$862,500**

59 Diluted EPS:
- Interest saved (net of tax) = $5m × 6% × (1 − 0.25) = $225,000
- Adjusted earnings = $3,000,000 + $225,000 = $3,225,000
- Adjusted shares = 10,000,000 + 1,200,000 = 11,200,000
- Diluted EPS = $3,225,000 / 11,200,000 = **28.8 cents**

60 **A and D**

61 Comparative EPS = 46.2 × (2.06/2.20) = 43.3 cents

Answer: **B — 43.3 cents per share**

SUBJECT F2 : ADVANCED FINANCIAL REPORTING

62 JKL, a listed entity, had 6 million $1 ordinary shares in issue on 1 January 20X3. On 28 February 20X3 JKL made a bonus issue of 1 new ordinary share for 4 held. On 1 July JKL then issued a further 1,500,000 new $1 ordinary shares at full market price. Reported basic earnings per share for the year ended 31 December 20X2 was 98.2 cents per share.

In the financial statements of JKL for the year to 31 December 20X3, what will the comparative figure for basic earnings per share be?

Give your answer in cents to one decimal place.

63 Options to purchase 1,500,000 $1 ordinary shares at $3.50 per share were issued on 1 January 20X2. These options are exercisable between 1 January 20X5 and 31 December 20X6. The average market value of each $1 ordinary share during the year ended 31 December 20X2 is $4.75.

The 'free' shares that should be added to the weighted average number of shares in the calculation of diluted earnings per share for the year ended 31 December 20X2 is:

- A   315,789
- B   394,737
- C   428,571
- D   535,714

IFRS® 16 *LEASES*

64 CR enters into a lease on 1 January 20X1 for a machine with a fair value of $235,000. CR will make annual payments in arrears of $70,000 over the four year lease term. The rate implicit in the lease is 9%.

Calculate the finance cost that should be recognised in the statement of profit or loss for the year ended 31 December 20X2 (the second year of the lease).

65 FL leases a machine to JS that would have a useful life of 8 years if bought outright.

Which THREE of the following independent characteristics would be likely to indicate that FL would treat the lease as a finance lease?

- A   The primary lease term is for four years and JS has the option to extend the term for a further four years for a small notional charge each year
- B   The FL is responsible for maintaining and repairing the machine in the event of a breakdown
- C   The machine is specialised in nature and has been built according to the specifications agreed by JS.
- D   At the end of the lease term, JS can purchase the asset at its then market value
- E   If JS cancels the lease before the end of the term it will be responsible for compensating FL for lost future rentals and interest

OBJECTIVE TEST QUESTIONS : SECTION 1

66 The table below provides a summary of accounting treatments prescribed by IFRS 16 *Leases* of sale and leaseback arrangements for lessees.

Sale and leaseback where the sale price of the asset is equal to fair value.	
Sale and leaseback where the sale price of the assets is above fair value.	
Sale and leaseback where the sale price is lower than the carrying amount.	
Sale and leaseback where the sale does not meet the requirements of a sale as per IFRS 15 *Revenue from contracts with customers*.	

Place ONE of the following options in each of the boxes above:

A	The asset is derecognised, a right-of-use asset is recorded and the difference between sale price and fair value is treated as additional financing
B	The asset remains on the statement of financial position and a financial liability is recorded
C	The asset is derecognised, a right-of-use asset is recorded and the difference between sale price and carrying amount is recognised as a prepayment in the statement of financial position.
D	The asset is derecognised, a right-of-use asset is recorded and the difference between sale price and carrying amount is recognised in profit or loss immediately

67 DF enters into a 10 year lease arrangement on 30 June 20X1 for portable fitness monitoring devices to grant to its employees as part of its internal wellbeing and corporate responsibility programme. Annual rental payments of $125,000 are to be paid however, as an incentive to the lessee, the first 12 months are rent free. The lease was considered to be for low value items by DF.

Calculate the charge to DF's statement of profit or loss in respect of the lease for the year ended 31 December 20X1.

68 LD enters into a lease on 1 January 20X1. Initial direct costs are $1,000. The lease term is five years and the interest rate implicit in the lease is 7%. The annual lease payments are $110,000 in arrears.

The non-current liability in respect of the above lease at 31 December 20X1 is:

A $288,650
B $290,312
C $372,570
D $373,890

17

SUBJECT F2 : ADVANCED FINANCIAL REPORTING

IFRS® 15 *REVENUE FROM CONTRACTS WITH CUSTOMERS*

69 Which of the following statements are true in relation to the recognition of revenue accordance with IFRS 15 *Revenue from contracts with customers*? Select all that apply:

- A A contract must exist between the seller and the buyer
- B Performance obligations must be fully satisfied
- C Variable consideration must be included in the value of the performance obligations provided
- D The goods have been delivered to the buyer
- E The entity must identify and separate the distinct performance obligations within a contract

70 WD operates a whisky distillery and its whisky takes on average ten years to mature. It finances this inventory holding period by entering into sale and repurchase agreements with its main bank.

In the year ended 31 March 20X5, it has sold $1,200,000 of inventory to the bank and entered into repurchase arrangements to buy the inventory back in ten years' time for $2,150,000. The cost of the inventory sold was $700,000 and WD has recognised profit of $500,000 in the statement of profit or loss for the year.

The directors have previously been happy to recognise sale and repurchase arrangements as loans, however they have decided this year that they want to recognise a sale and profit instead, in order to boost profits and the share price. They are all members of an executive share option scheme that is due to vest next year and their options will then become exercisable.

Which one of the following statements in respect of this arrangement is true?

- A As long as the transaction is recorded as a purchase of inventory in ten years' time, the proposed treatment is in accordance with international financial reporting standards
- B It is acceptable to recognise the profit now as the repurchase is a significant length of time away
- C It is acceptable to recognise the profit now as WD is not looking to raise any equity or debt finance and therefore it is not misleading any stakeholders
- D The directors are considering their own interests over and above those of the shareholders and are therefore not acting in accordance with their professional and ethical responsibilities

71 ST enters into a contract to develop bespoke software for a customer. Having completed development and delivered the software to the customer on 30 June 20X3, ST has invoiced the customer the agreed fixed fee of $575,000, comprising $500,000 for the development of the software and $75,000 for service and support of the software over the 3-year support period.

The revenue that should be recognised in ST's statement of profit or loss for the year ended 31 December 20X3 in respect of the above customer contract is:

A $500,000

B $512,500

C $525,000

D $575,000

72 JK is a motor dealership and has motor vehicles on its premises that were supplied by a car manufacturer, SB. Trading between JK and SB was subject to a contractual arrangement.

Which one of the following would be an indicator that SB should continue to recognise the motor vehicles in its inventory?

A When JK makes a sale, SB raises an invoice to JK at the price agreed when the vehicle is delivered to JK

B JK has the right to return any vehicle at any time without incurring a penalty

C JK is responsible for insuring all the vehicles on its premises

D JK is entitled to use any of the vehicles supplied to it for demonstration purposes and road testing

73 On 31 May 20X1, DRT sold land to NKL, an entity that provides DRT with long-term finance. The sale price was $1,600,000 and the carrying amount of the land on the date of sale was $1,310,000 (the original cost of the land). Under the terms of the sale agreement DRT has the option to repurchase the land within the next four years for between $1,660,000 and $1,800,000 depending on the date of repurchase. NKL cannot use the land for any purpose without the prior consent of DRT. The land must be repurchased for $1,800,000 at the end of the four year period if the option is not exercised before that time.

Which one of the following statements is true in respect of the sale of land?

A DRT should continue to recognised the land in its financial statements in the period between 31 May 20X1 and the date of repurchase

B DRT should derecognise the land on 31 May 20X1 and record a profit on disposal of $290,000

C DRT should derecognise the land on 31 May 20X1 but should defer recognition of the profit on disposal and recognise it over the next four years

D DRT should only derecognise the land if it is considered likely that it will exercise the option to repurchase over the next four years

74 XZ sells goods to WY on a sale or return basis. The terms of the arrangement are that the goods can be returned within 28 days of sale if WY has not managed to sell them on. The total value of sales made to WY still within the 28 day sale or return period at 31 December 20X2, XZ's reporting date, is $1,250,000. WY has confirmed that 38% of these goods are still held in inventory at 31 December 20X2. XZ has made a margin of 25% on the sales.

Which of the following statements is true in respect of the above?

A   If it is considered likely that WY will manage to sell the remaining products on, all of the revenue can be recognised in the year ended 31 December 20X2

B   No revenue should be recognised on any of the sale or return items until the 28 day period has expired

C   XZ should recognise $775,000 in revenue in the year ended 31 December 20X2

D   XZ should still recognise $380,000 of the goods delivered to WY in inventory at 31 December 20X2

75 BL commenced a fixed price contract on 1 March 20X1 to construct a building on land controlled by their customer. The contract is scheduled to run for three years and the total contract price is $40 million.

The details of the contract at the reporting dates of 31 December 20X1 and 20X2 are:

Year ended 31 December:	20X1	20X2
	$m	$m
Costs incurred to date	7	18
Expected costs to complete	26	16
Cumulative work certified as complete	8	22

BL uses output methods based on work certified as complete to calculate the stage of completion.

Calculate the profit that BL would recognise on the above contract in the year ended 31 December 20X2. State your answer in $m to one decimal place.

76 VY has a contract to construct an asset on behalf of their customer in progress at its reporting date of 31 December 20X4. Revenue should be recorded over time for this contract. The details of the contract are as follows:

	To date	In current year
	$000	$000
Profit recognised in statement of profit or loss	1,700	1,300
Costs incurred to date	5,100	4,000
Progress billings	6,000	6,000

The balance that should appear in VY's statement of financial position at 31 December 20X4 is:

A $700,000 contract asset
B $700,000 contract liabilities
C $800,000 contract asset
D $800,000 contract liabilities

77 DB commenced a contract to construct a specialised asset on 1 January 20X5 and the details at its reporting date of 31 December 20X5 are as follows:

	$000
Total contract price	3,000
Costs incurred to date:	
Attributable to work completed	1,500
Inventory purchased, not yet used	150
Expected costs to complete	350
Progress billings	900

DB uses input methods to assess progress of the contract, specifically the percentage of costs incurred to total expected costs to calculate the stage of completion of construction contracts. DB has the legal right for repayment for work performed to date.

The profit that should be recognised in DB's statement of profit or loss for the year ended 31 December 20X5, to the nearest $000, is:

A $300,000

B $750,000

C $811,000

D $825,000

78 NM commenced a two year contract to construct an office building on 1 April 20X4. The contract had a fixed price of $26 million. NM incurred costs to 31 March 20X5, its reporting date, of $17 million and has now estimated that a further $11 million will need to be incurred to complete the contract. The work certified as complete at 31 March 20X5 is $14 million and progress billings of $12 million have been made.

NM uses work certified as a percentage of contract price to calculate the progress to completion of the contract.

Which THREE of the following statements are true in respect of the above contract in NM's financial statements for the year ended 31 March 20X5?

A   Cost of sales of $16 million should be recognised

B   Cost of sales of $17 million should be recognised

C   Revenue of $14 million should be recognised

D   Revenue of $15 million should be recognised

E   The statement of financial position should reflect a contract asset balance of $3 million

F   The statement of financial position should reflect a contract liability of $7 million

SUBJECT F2 : ADVANCED FINANCIAL REPORTING

IAS® 37 PROVISIONS, CONTINGENT LIABILITIES AND CONTINGENT ASSETS

79 Which one of the following costs would not be recognised in accordance with IAS 37 *Provisions, contingent liabilities and contingent assets*?

    A   Expected costs of warranty repairs for goods sold under warranty prior to the reporting date

    B   Costs relating to closure of a division that has been announced prior to the reporting date

    C   Expected losses over the next 12 months from a subsidiary acquired a week before the reporting date

    D   Remaining lease payments after vacating premises that cannot be sublet

80 ES operates in the oil and gas industry and publishes an environmental and social report to demonstrate its corporate social responsibility. It is partly responsible for a recent oil leak causing damage to the local environment and is planning to voluntarily contribute to the costs of the clean-up, although it is under no legal obligation to do so. It anticipates the cost to be $500,000 but this is not certain.

Which one of the following statements is true in respect of this scenario?

    A   Under no circumstances should a provision be made in the financial statements of ES as there is no legal obligation to incur the expenditure

    B   There is a probable outflow of economic benefit but the timing and amount is uncertain and so a contingent liability should be included in ES's financial statements

    C   A provision should be made for the clean-up costs because ES are planning to incur the expenditure and this will result in an outflow of economic benefits

    D   A provision should be made for the clean-up costs if ES has created a valid expectation that it will incur the expenditure in its publication of the environmental and social report

81 IAS 37 *Provisions, contingent liabilities and contingent assets* sets criteria that must be satisfied before a provision is made or a contingent item disclosed. The accounting treatment can be summarised as follows:

Degree of probability of an outflow/inflow of resources	Liability	Asset
Virtually certain	Recognise	
Probable		
Possible		
Remote		Ignore

Place ONE of the following options in each of the shaded boxes above:

Disclose (in note)	Ignore
Make provision	Recognise

Note that each option may be used more than once.

OBJECTIVE TEST QUESTIONS : SECTION 1

IAS® 12 TAXATION

82 Which TWO of the following would result in a deferred tax asset?

- A A provision for warranty costs, that are tax deductible when incurred
- B Development costs capitalised in the statement of financial position, for which a tax deduction has already been claimed
- C Losses to be carried forward and offset against future expected profits
- D Property, plant and equipment with a carrying amount greater than the tax base
- E Revaluation surplus on land and buildings

83 At 1 January 20X3 SD had a deferred tax liability brought forward of $25,000 resulting from temporary differences on property, plant and equipment. At 31 December 20X3 the carrying amount of property, plant and equipment in SD's statement of financial position was $470,000 and its tax base was $365,000. The corporate income tax rate was 20%.

The impact of deferred tax in the statement of profit or loss for the year ended 31 December 20X3 is:

- A $4,000 charge
- B $4,000 credit
- C $21,000 charge
- D $21,000 credit

84 HT has an item of property, plant and equipment with a carrying amount of $400,000 and a tax base of $370,000 at 31 December 20X5. The corporate income tax rate is 20%. The deferred tax liability brought forward in respect of this property, plant and equipment is $4,000.

HT then implements a revaluation policy for the first time and revalues the property, plant and equipment to $750,000.

Which THREE of the following statements are true in respect of HT's deferred tax on the above property, plant and equipment?

- A An additional temporary difference of $70,000 is created by the revaluation
- B The balance on the revaluation reserve will be $280,000
- C The deferred tax liability after the revaluation is $76,000
- D The overall charge to profit or loss in respect of deferred tax on the property, plant and equipment in the year will be $2,000
- E The overall charge to profit or loss in respect of deferred tax on the property, plant and equipment in the year will be $72,000
- F The revaluation has no impact on deferred tax as it does not affect the tax base

SUBJECT F2 : ADVANCED FINANCIAL REPORTING

85 QW prepares its financial statements to 31 December each year. On 1 January 20X1 QW set up a share option scheme for the benefit of its employees and recognised an expense in the statement of profit or loss in accordance with IFRS 2 *Share-based payment*. The vesting period is three years.

When recognising deferred tax for the year ended 31 December 20X1 QW should:

- A recognise a deferred tax liability in relation to the share option scheme to reflect the future tax consequence when the options are exercised
- B ignore the share option scheme as there is no asset or liability recognised in the statement of financial position and therefore no temporary difference
- C recognise a deferred tax asset that reflects the tax deduction that can be claimed when the options are exercised
- D recognise a deferred tax asset that equates to the expense recognised in the statement of profit or loss multiplied by the tax rate

86 Complete the sentences below by placing one of the following options in each of the spaces.

| deductible | asset |
| taxable | liability |

If the carrying amount of an asset exceeds its tax base then there is a _____ temporary difference and this will result in a deferred tax _____.

IAS® 24 RELATED PARTIES

87 Which THREE of the following would be considered related parties of CV, in accordance with IAS 24 *Related Party Disclosures*?

- A A shareholder who owns 25% of the ordinary shares of CV
- B A subsidiary of CV, with whom CV does not trade
- C CV's biggest customer, providing 60% of CV's annual revenue
- D CV's main supplier of finance, providing significant loans to the business
- E The employees of CV
- F The spouse of CV's managing director

88 AB owns 80% of CD. CD owns 40% of EF, over which it exercises significant influence. AB also shares joint control of a JV, a separate entity, with PQ via a joint arrangement.

Which one of the following sets would be considered related parties of AB, in accordance with international financial reporting standards?

- A CD, EF and PQ
- B CD, EF and JV
- C CD, JV and PQ
- D CD, EF, JV and PQ

OBJECTIVE TEST QUESTIONS : SECTION 1

FINANCIAL REPORTING (II)

CONSOLIDATED FINANCIAL STATEMENTS

BASIC GROUPS

89 LP is considering selling one of its wholly owned subsidiaries, GH, after the current year end however it is concerned that it will struggle to find a buyer due to GH's poor profitability. LP uses GH as a supplier and therefore has decided to increase its purchase prices in the final three months of the accounting period in order to boost GH's profits. As LP already trades with GH it does not believe that any additional disclosures need to be made to reflect this revised pricing.

It intends to recover the increase in cost by arranging a significant dividend payment prior to the disposal but after the year end.

Which one of the following statements in respect of this arrangement is true?

- A Any inter-group transactions are eliminated in the consolidated financial statements and therefore this does not create an ethical issue
- B As the cost will be recovered via the dividend payment there is no ethical issue
- C It is a deliberate attempt to mislead potential acquirers who might rely on GH's financial statements and as a result the directors are acting unethically
- D The proposed accounting treatment is in accordance with international financial reporting standards and therefore there is no ethical issue

90 Which one of the following statements is INCORRECT in respect of the recognition of goodwill in consolidated financial statements?

- A If goodwill at acquisition is negative, it should be credited to profit or loss immediately
- B Changes in the fair value of the subsidiary's net assets arising after acquisition are dealt with as post-acquisition adjustments in line with group accounting policies
- C Contingent consideration should only be recognised in the goodwill calculation if it is considered probable that it will be paid
- D The various elements of consideration paid should be measured at their fair value at the date of acquisition

The following scenario relates to questions 91 to 92 (2 questions)

RF acquired 80% of the ordinary shares of YT on 1 January 20X1. The book value of YT's net assets at 1 January 20X1 was $850,000 and the fair value of the net assets of YT was considered to be the same as book value at this date with the following exceptions:

- The fair value of property, plant and equipment was $650,000 higher than book value. These assets were assessed to have a remaining useful life of 5 years from the date of acquisition.
- The fair value of inventories was considered to be $25,000 higher than book value. All of the inventories were sold by 31 December 20X1.
- YT had disclosed a contingent liability in the notes to its financial statements. The fair value of this was considered to be $100,000 at acquisition and the fair value at 31 December 20X1 was $110,000.

RF is preparing the consolidated financial statements for the year ended 31 December 20X1.

SUBJECT F2 : ADVANCED FINANCIAL REPORTING

91 The fair value of net assets that would be reflected in the calculation of goodwill arising on the acquisition of YT in RF's consolidated financial statements is:

- A $1,295,000
- B $1,400,000
- C $1,415,000
- D $1,425,000

92 Which one of the following statements is true in respect of how the above would be reflected in RF's consolidated financial statements for the year ended 31 December 20X1?

- A Additional depreciation of $130,000 would be charged in the consolidated statement of profit or loss
- B The contingent liability would be recognised as a liability of $100,000 in the consolidated statement of financial position
- C The increase in fair value of the contingent liability between acquisition and the reporting date should be recognised as a post-acquisition adjustment to goodwill
- D The $25,000 difference between book value and fair value of inventory would result in an additional credit to consolidated profit or loss when the inventory is sold

---

The following scenario relates to questions 93 to 95 (3 questions)

MX acquired 80% of the 1 million issued $1 ordinary share capital of FZ on 1 April 20X9 for $1,750,000 when FZ's retained earnings were $920,000.

The carrying amount of FZ's net assets was considered to be the same as the fair value at the date of acquisition with the exception of FZ's machinery, which had a carrying amount of $680,000 and a fair value of $745,000 on 1 April 20X9. The remaining useful life of the machinery was estimated at 5 years from the date of acquisition.

MX depreciates all assets on a straight line basis over their estimated lives on a monthly basis.

FZ sold goods to MX with a sales value of $300,000 during the 9 months since the acquisition. All of these goods remain in MX's inventories at the reporting date. FZ makes 20% gross profit margin on all sales.

The retained earnings reported in the financial statements of MX and FZ as at 31 December 20X9 are $3.2 million and $1.1 million respectively. There has been no impairment to goodwill since the date of acquisition.

The group policy is to measure non-controlling interest (NCI) at fair value at the date of acquisition. The fair value of the NCI at 1 April 20X9 was $320,000.

---

93 Calculate the carrying amount of goodwill that would be recognised in the consolidated statement of financial position of the MX Group at 31 December 20X9 (to the nearest $000).

94 The NCI to be included in the equity section of the consolidated statement of financial position of the MX group at 31 December 20X9 will be:

- A $341,400
- B $342,050
- C $354,050
- D $419,050

OBJECTIVE TEST QUESTIONS : SECTION 1

95   Which THREE of the following statements are true in respect of the consolidated retained earnings to be included in the consolidated statement of financial position of the MX Group for the year ended 31 December 20X9?

A   It will include 100% of MX's retained earnings

B   80% of FZ's post-acquisition earnings will be debited to it

C   The impact of the unrealised profit adjustment on it will be $60,000

D   The impact of the fair value adjustment on it will be $7,800

E   Both the unrealised profit adjustment and the fair value adjustment will cause a reduction in it

96   JK acquired 75% of the 500,000 $1 equity shares of LM on 1 January 20X2 for $1,200,000 when the fair value of LM's net assets was $1,100,000. At the date of acquisition the balance on LM's reserves was $350,000 and the only fair value adjustment required was in relation to a property with a remaining useful life at acquisition of ten years.

The carrying amount of property, plant and equipment in the individual financial statements of JK and LM at 31 December 20X2, the reporting date, are $3,300,000 and $850,000 respectively.

Calculate the carrying amount of property, plant and equipment that would be shown in the consolidated statement of financial position of the JK group at 31 December 20X2. State your answer to the nearest $000.

97   AB acquired an 80% investment in XY on 1 January 20X1. The consideration consisted of the following:

- The transfer of 500,000 shares in AB with a nominal value of $1.00 each and a market value on the date of acquisition of $3.50 each

- $408,000 of cash paid on 1 January 20X1; and

- $1,000,000 of cash, payable on 1 January 20X3 (a discount rate of 9% has been used to value the liability in the financial statements of AB).

AB also paid legal and professional fees in respect of the acquisition of $150,000.

The best estimate of the fair value of the consideration to be included in the calculation of goodwill arising on the acquisition of XY is:

A $1,750,000

B $3,000,000

C $3,150,000

D $3,158,000

98   AB acquired 80% of CD's 500,000 ordinary shares for $620,000 on 1 January 20X7 when the fair value of CD's net assets was $680,000. The market price of CD's ordinary shares at 1 January 20X7 was $1.80.

The directors of AB are trying to decide whether to measure the non-controlling interest of CD at fair value or the proportionate share of the fair value of net assets at acquisition.

Calculate the ADDITIONAL goodwill that would be recognised if the directors choose the fair value method over the proportionate method. State your answer to the nearest $.

SUBJECT F2 : ADVANCED FINANCIAL REPORTING

99 Complete the following sentences by placing one of the options identified below in each of the spaces.

| arrangement | entity |
| operation | venture |

A joint _____ is an arrangement of which two parties or more have joint control.
A joint _____ is where the parties that have joint control have rights to the assets, and obligations for the liabilities, relating to the arrangement. A joint _____ is where the parties that have joint control have rights to the net assets of the arrangement.

The following scenario relates to questions 100 to 102 (3 questions)

ZB acquired 70% of the 1 million issued $1 ordinary shares of HD on 1 January 20X3 for $3,250,000 when HD's retained earnings were $1,500,000. ZB has no other subsidiaries.

The carrying amount of HD's net assets was considered to be the same as the fair value at the date of acquisition with the exception of HD's non-depreciable property. The book value of these assets was $1,200,000 and their fair value was $1,600,000.

The group policy is to measure non-controlling interest at fair value at the acquisition date. The fair value of the non-controlling interest in HD was $1,325,000 on 1 January 20X3.

An impairment review performed on 31 December 20X4 indicated that goodwill on the acquisition of HD had been impaired by $425,000. No impairment was recognised in the year ended 31 December 20X3. The retained earnings of HD at 31 December 20X4 were $2,750,000.

100 The goodwill that will be recorded in non-current assets of the ZB group as at 31 December 20X4 is:

    A $795,000
    B $1,250,000
    C $1,650,000
    D $1,675,000

101 Which TWO of the following statements are INCORRECT in respect of the consolidated retained earnings of the ZB group at 31 December 20X4?

    A   70% of HD's post-acquisition retained earnings will be credited to it
    B   100% of ZB's retained earnings will be included in it
    C   It will be affected by the fair value adjustment arising at the date of acquisition
    D   Goodwill impairment of $297,500 will be deducted in it
    E   Goodwill impairment of $425,000 will be deducted in it

102 The non-controlling interest to be included in the consolidated statement of financial position of the ZB group at 31 December 20X4 will be:

    A $1,117,500
    B $1,245,000
    C $1,572,500
    D $1,700,000

103 BC acquired 65% of the ordinary share capital of FG, its only subsidiary, on 1 January 20X3. In the year ended 31 December 20X3 FG had total comprehensive income of $125,000. A fair value adjustment at acquisition resulted in additional depreciation of $30,000 being charged to consolidated profit or loss in the year ended 31 December 20X3.

The directors of BC carried out an impairment review on the goodwill arising on the acquisition of FG at 31 December 20X3 and considered it to have been impaired by $15,000.

It is group policy to measure non-controlling interest at fair value at the date of acquisition.

The share of post-acquisition reserves of FG that would be included in the consolidated reserves of the BC group at 31 December 20X3 is:

A $52,000

B $61,750

C $71,500

D $81,250

104 XZ owns 35% of the equity share capital of TY. During the year to 31 December 20X1 XZ purchased goods with a sales value of $200,000 from TY. Half of these goods remained in XZ's inventories at the year ended 31 December 20X1. TY makes a gross profit margin of 25% on all sales.

Which of the following accounting adjustments would XZ process in the preparation of its consolidated financial statements in relation to these goods?

A	Dr	Share of profit of associate	$7,000	Cr	Inventories	$7,000
B	Dr	Cost of sales	$7,000	Cr	Investment in associate	$7,000
C	Dr	Share of profit of associate	$8,750	Cr	Inventories	$8,750
D	Dr	Cost of sales	$8,750	Cr	Investment in associate	$8,750

105 Which THREE of the following statements are true in respect of the recognition of non-controlling interests in consolidated financial statements?

A   Directors are free to choose from two methods for measuring non-controlling interests at acquisition and can choose different methods for different subsidiaries within the same group

B   Goodwill impairment will always affect the non-controlling interest

C   Provisions for unrealised profits on transactions between entities within the same group will always affect the non-controlling interest

D   The non-controlling interest is initially recognised at acquisition by debiting goodwill and crediting equity

E   The non-controlling interest's share of any dividend paid by a subsidiary is eliminated upon consolidation

F   The non-controlling interest will always be reduced by their share of any additional depreciation charge arising from fair value adjustments to a subsidiary's non-current assets at acquisition

106 AB acquired 80% of the ordinary share capital of CD, its only subsidiary, on 1 October 20X8. In the year ended 30 June 20X9 CD had total comprehensive income of $90,000. A fair value adjustment at acquisition resulted in additional depreciation of $20,000 being charged to profit or loss in the year ended 30 June 20X9.

The directors of AB carried out an impairment review on the goodwill arising on the acquisition of CD at 30 June 20X9 and considered it to have been impaired by $30,000.

AB sold goods to CD on 1 May 20X9 with a sales value of $80,000. Half of these goods remain in CD's inventories at 30 June 20X9. AB makes a 25% gross profit margin on all sales.

It is group policy to measure non-controlling interest at fair value at the date of acquisition. Profit is assumed to accrue evenly throughout the year.

The share of total comprehensive income attributable to the non-controlling interest for the year ended 30 June 20X9 is:

A $1,500
B $3,500
C $6,000
D $8,000

107 PA owns 80% of the ordinary share capital of SU, its only subsidiary. It is group policy to measure non-controlling interest at fair value at the date of acquisition.

When calculating the total comprehensive income attributable to the non-controlling interest each year, the subsidiary's profit must be adjusted for which of the following transactions?

Select ALL that apply.

A   Profit on the sale of goods by PA to SU, where SU still holds the goods at the reporting date
B   Profit on the sale of goods by SU to PA, where PA still holds the goods at the reporting date
C   Impairment to the goodwill arising on the acquisition of SU
D   Additional depreciation arising from a fair value adjustment made to SU's net assets at the date of acquisition
E   Elimination of dividend paid by SU to PA

108 SA acquired 75% of the ordinary shares of TR on 1 August 20X3 for $2,200,000. At the date of acquisition the book value of TR's net assets was $1,220,000 and this was considered to equal fair value with the exception of property, plant and equipment. The fair value of property, plant and equipment was $475,000 higher than book value and had an estimated useful life of 20 years from the date of acquisition. TR is SA's only subsidiary.

It is group policy to measure non-controlling interest at its proportionate share of the fair value of the net assets at the date of acquisition.

The book value of TR's net assets at 31 July 20X7, the reporting date, is $2,500,000.

Goodwill arising on the acquisition of TR had been impaired by $150,000 at 31 July 20X7.

Calculate the non-controlling interest balance that would appear in the consolidated statement of financial position of the SA group as at 31 July 20X7. State your answer to the nearest $.

OBJECTIVE TEST QUESTIONS : **SECTION 1**

109 ER acquired 80% of the equity share capital of MR on 1 January 20X0 for $2,000,000 when the retained earnings of MR were $1,200,000. At the date of acquisition the fair value of the net assets of MR was the same as the book value with the exception of property, plant and equipment. The fair value of property, plant and equipment was $400,000 higher than book value. Property, plant and equipment had an estimated useful life of 10 years from the date of acquisition.

The carrying amount of property, plant and equipment in the individual financial statements of ER and MR at 31 December 20X2, the reporting date, were $5,900,000 and $2,000,000 respectively.

Calculate the carrying amount of property, plant and equipment that would be presented in the consolidated statement of financial position of the ER Group as at 31 December 20X2.

Give your answer to the nearest $000.

110 YG acquired 75% of the ordinary share capital of VB, its only subsidiary, on 1 July 20X6. In the year ended 31 December 20X6 VB made total profit of $180,000. A fair value adjustment at acquisition resulted in additional depreciation of $15,000 being charged to profit or loss in the post-acquisition period.

VB sold goods to YG on 1 November 20X6 with a sales value of $100,000. 30% of these goods remain in YG's inventories at 31 December 20X6. VB makes a 30% gross profit margin on all sales.

The directors carried out an impairment review on the goodwill arising on the acquisition of VB at 31 December 20X6 and charged $25,000 to consolidated profit or loss as a result.

It is group policy to measure non-controlling interest at the proportionate share of the fair value of net assets at the date of acquisition. Profit is assumed to accrue evenly throughout the year.

The profit attributable to the non-controlling interest for the year ended 31 December 20X6 is:

A $10,250
B $12,500
C $16,500
D $18,750

111 Brendan bought 30% of WeeJoe on 1 July 20X4. Brendan is deemed to exert significant influence over WeeJoe and already owns other investments in subsidiaries. WeeJoe's statement of profit or loss for the year shows a profit of $600,000. WeeJoe paid a dividend to Brendan of $75,000 on 1 December 20X4.

Since the 1st July 20X4, WeeJoe has sold goods to Brendan with a sales value of $25,000. WeeJoe uses a mark-up on cost of 25%. By the year end, 20% of these goods have been sold on by Brendan.

At the year end, the investment in WeeJoe was judged to have been impaired by $15,000.

What will be shown under 'Share of profit from associate' in Brendan's consolidated statement of profit or loss for the year ended 31 December 20X4?

A $71,000
B $73,800
C $75,000
D $86,000
E $165,000

SUBJECT F2 : ADVANCED FINANCIAL REPORTING

112 Dolph bought 20% of Chuck on 1 January 20X8, when Chuck had share capital of $1,000,000 $1 shares and $4,000,000 retained earnings. Dolph exerts significant influence over Chuck and already prepares consolidated accounts.

Dolph paid by giving the previous owners of Chuck, 1 Dolph share for every 4 shares bought in Chuck. At the date of acquisition, Dolph's shares had a market value of $4.50 and Chuck's had a market value of $2.

At 31 December 20X8, Chuck's net assets were $4,600,000. At the year-end, Dolph considered the investment in Chuck to be impaired by $100,000.

During the year, Dolph sells goods at a price of $200,000 to Chuck making a total profit of $50,000. All of these goods remain in the inventory of Chuck as at the year-end.

What is the value shown under 'Investment in Associate' in the consolidated statement of financial position as at 31 December 20X8?

- A $20,000
- B $35,000
- C $115,000
- D $195,000

COMPLEX GROUPS (INDIRECT HOLDINGS)

113 AZ acquired 80% of the ordinary share capital of B on 1 January 20X0 for $800 million.

B acquired 60% of the ordinary share capital of C on 1 January 20X1 for $480 million. At 1 January 20X1 the fair value of the non-controlling in C, included in the consolidated financial statements of AZ, was $280 million.

The group policy is to value non-controlling interest (NCI) at fair value at the date of acquisition.

The fair value of the net assets of C was $620m on 1 January 20X1.

Calculate the goodwill arising on the acquisition of C in the consolidated financial statements of the AZ group. State your answer to the nearest $m.

114 AQ acquired 80% of the equity share capital of B on 1 January 20X3. B acquired 60% of the equity share capital of C on 1 January 20X2.

Which TWO of the following statements in respect of the consolidated financial statements of the AQ Group for the year ended 31 December 20X3 are true?

- A C will be equity accounted because AQ has an effective interest of 48% in C
- B 100% of the carrying amount of property, plant and equipment of both B and C will be included in the statement of financial position
- C C will be recognised as a subsidiary of the AQ group from 1 January 20X2
- D AQ controls both B and C and both will be consolidated as subsidiaries from 1 January 20X3
- E 60% of the post-acquisition retained earnings of C will be included within consolidated reserves

115 BV owns 75% of the equity share capital of D. D owns 60% of the equity share capital of M. Both investments have been held for a number of years. The profits for the year for D and M were $87,000 and $70,000 respectively. There are no other entities in the BV group.

All three entities paid a dividend to their ordinary shareholders in the year. BV paid a dividend of $80,000, D paid a dividend of $50,000 and M paid a dividend of $20,000.

The profit attributable to non-controlling interest that will be reported in the consolidated statement of profit or loss of the BV group will be:

- A $46,750
- B $49,750
- C $57,250
- D $60,250

116 FG has owned 75% of the equity shares of ED since 1 January 20X5. ED has owned 60% of the equity shares of CA since 1 January 20X3.

The balance on CA's retained earnings was as follows:

	$000
1 January 20X3	4,500
1 January 20X5	5,600
31 December 20X6	8,000

Calculate the amount that would be included in the consolidated retained earnings of the FG group at 31 December 20X6 in respect of CA. Give your answer to the nearest $000.

117 AB owns 60% of the equity shares of CD and 30% of the equity shares of EF. CD also owns 30% of the equity shares of EF. All of the shareholdings were acquired on the same date.

Which one of the following statements in respect of the consolidated financial statements of the AB Group is true?

- A EF is an associate of the group as both AB and CD can exercise significant influence via their 30% holdings
- B EF is an associate of the AB group because the effective interest of AB in EF's results is 48%
- C 48% of EF's post-acquisition reserves should be recognised in the consolidated reserves of the AB group
- D An indirect holding adjustment would be applied in the calculation of goodwill based on 52% of CD's investment in EF

118 XZ acquired 80% of the equity share capital of WV on 1 January 20X3. WV acquired 65% of the equity share capital of ST on 1 January 20X4 for $450,000 when the reserves of ST were $275,000. The fair value of the non-controlling interest in ST at 1 January 20X4, reflecting the XZ group's effective holding, was $300,000. It is group policy to measure non-controlling interests at fair value at acquisition.

At the reporting date of 31 December 20X6, ST had reserves of $580,000.

The amount that would appear in the equity section of the XZ group's consolidated statement of financial position at 31 December 20X6 in respect of the non-controlling interest in ST is:

A $230,400
B $356,400
C $446,400
D $458,600

119 PB acquired 80% of the 100,000 $1 equity shares of SD on 1 July 20X5. SD then acquired 60% of equity shares of TW on 1 January 20X7 for $35,000 when TW's net assets were $36,400. The book value of TW's net assets at acquisition is considered to be the same as fair value.

It is group policy to measure the non-controlling interest (NCI) at fair value at acquisition. The fair value of the NCI in TW, based on PB's effective holding, at 1 January 20X7 was $31,000.

Goodwill has been tested for impairment and none is considered to have arisen as at 31 December 20X7.

The goodwill on the acquisition of TW that would appear as part of total goodwill in the consolidated statement of financial position of the PB group at 31 December 20X7 is:

A $11,400
B $12,800
C $22,600
D $29,600

120 DG acquired 60% of the equity shares of LM on 1 January 20X1. LM had previously acquired 60% of the equity shares of FG.

Which TWO of the following statements in respect of the consolidated financial statements of the DG Group are FALSE?

A DG will consolidate both LM and FG from 1 January 20X1 onwards
B FG will be recognised as an associate as DG's effective holding is 36%
C Non-controlling interest with an effective holding of 64% will be recognised in relation to the investment of the DG group in FG
D When calculating goodwill on the acquisition of FG, only 36% of the amount paid by LM should be included as the consideration paid
E When calculating goodwill on the acquisition of FG, only 60% of the amount paid by LM should be included as the consideration paid

OBJECTIVE TEST QUESTIONS : **SECTION 1**

CHANGES IN GROUP STRUCTURE

121 SD acquired 1,600,000 of the 2,000,000 $1 ordinary shares in JH on 1 March 20X6 for $2,800,000. The retained earnings of JH at the date of acquisition were $1,000,000 and the carrying amount of JH's net assets was considered to be the same as fair value. The fair value of the non-controlling interest (NCI) in JH at acquisition was $680,000 and it is group policy to value NCI at fair value at acquisition. There has been no goodwill impairment.

On 1 October 20X8, SD sold 1,000,000 of the shares in JH for $2,500,000. The fair value of the remaining holding at this date was $1,200,000. The retained earnings of JH at 1 October 20X8 were $1,300,000.

The gain or loss on disposal recognised in SD's consolidated statement of profit or loss on disposal of the JH shares on 1 October 20X8 will be calculated as follows:

Gain or loss on disposal	$000
Sale proceeds	2,500
Fair value of remaining holding	
Net assets at disposal	(3,300)
Goodwill at disposal	(480)
NCI at disposal	
	————
Gain/(loss) on disposal	
	————

Place ONE of the following values in each of the highlighted boxes in the above table:

VALUES	
660	(660)
680	(680)
740	(740)
820	(820)
1,200	(1,200)
1,300	(1,300)

122 At 1 January 20X4 FR owned 75% of the ordinary share capital of MA. On 1 April 20X4 FR acquired a further 15% of MA's ordinary share capital for $130,000.

Which one of the following statements in respect of the purchase of the additional shares in FG on 1 April 20X4 is INCORRECT?

A No goodwill arises on the acquisition of the additional shares in the consolidated financial statements of the FR group

B The acquisition of additional shares results in a transfer between owners and is recognised in the consolidated statement of changes in equity of the FR group

C The reduction in non-controlling interest will be 15% of the balance on the non-controlling interest reserve at 1 April 20X4

D There will be an adjustment in FR's consolidated reserves to reflect the difference between the consideration paid and the reduction in the non-controlling interest

35

SUBJECT F2 : ADVANCED FINANCIAL REPORTING

123 RBE owns 70% of the ordinary share capital of DCA at 31 December 20X0. RBE purchases a further 20% of the ordinary share capital of DCA on 1 October 20X1 for $540,000. The carrying amount of NCI immediately prior to the change in shareholding was $755,000.

Dividends were paid by both group entities in April 20X1. The dividends paid by RBE and DCA were $200,000 and $100,000 respectively.

Place the correct amounts in respect of the additional purchase or use 'BLANK' in order to reflect the impact on the consolidated statement of changes in equity for the RBE Group for the year ended 31 December 20X1.

Extract from the consolidated statement of changes in equity for RBE Group for the year ended 31 December 20X1

	Attributable to equity holders of parent	Attributable to non-controlling interest
	$000	$000
Balance at start of year	3,350	650
Comprehensive income for the year	1,280	150
Dividends paid	(200)	
Adjustment to NCI for additional purchase of DCA shares		
Adjustment to parent's equity for additional purchase of DCA shares		

VALUES	
10	(10)
30	(30)
37	(37)
67	(67)
473	(473)
503	(503)
BLANK	

124 YU acquired 90% of JK some years ago for $600,000. Goodwill arising on the acquisition was $80,000 and there has been no impairment since acquisition. It is group policy to measure non-controlling interest at the date of acquisition at fair value.

On 30 June 20X5 YU disposed of a third of its investment in JK for $400,000. At this date the carrying amount of the net assets of JK in the consolidated financial statements of the YU group was $800,000.

Calculate the amount that will be credited to the YU group's equity reserves upon disposal of the shares on 30 June 20X5. State your answer to the nearest $.

OBJECTIVE TEST QUESTIONS : SECTION 1

125 SD acquired 60% of the 1 million $1 ordinary shares of KL on 1 July 20X0 for $3,250,000 when KL's reserves were $2,760,000. The group policy is to measure non-controlling interest (NCI) at fair value at the date of acquisition. The fair value of the NCI at 1 July 20X0 was $1,960,000. There has been no impairment of goodwill since the date of acquisition.

SD acquired a further 20% of KL's share capital on 1 March 20X1 for $1,000,000 when the reserves of SD were $3,240,000.

The accounting entry to record the acquisition of the additional 20% investment in KL in the consolidated financial statements of the SD Group is:

A	Dr	Bank	$1,000,000
	Dr	Group reserves	$76,000
	Cr	NCI	$1,076,000
B	Dr	Bank	$1,000,000
	Dr	Profit for the year	$76,000
	Cr	NCI	$1,076,000
C	Dr	NCI	$1,076,000
	Cr	Profit for the year	$76,000
	Cr	Bank	$1,000,000
D	Dr	NCI	$1,076,000
	Cr	Group reserves	$76,000
	Cr	Bank	$1,000,000

126 SOT disposed of 40,000 $1 ordinary shares in UV on 1 July 20X9 for $960,000 when UV's reserves were $1,800,000. SOT had originally acquired 75,000 of the 100,000 $1 issued ordinary share capital of UV for $980,000 on 1 November 20X6, when the balance on UV's reserves was $1,020,000. No fair value adjustments were considered necessary to UV's net assets at the date of acquisition. The fair value of the shareholding retained at 1 July 20X9 was $792,000.

The group policy is to value the non-controlling interest at the proportionate share of the fair value of the net assets at the date of acquisition. Goodwill has been fully impaired.

Calculate the gain that would be recorded in the consolidated statement of profit or loss of the SOT Group upon disposal of the shares in UV on 1 July 20X9.

Give your answer to the nearest $000.

127 AB acquired 70% of the ordinary share capital of CD on 1 January 20X2 for $6,200,000. AB then purchased a further 10% of the ordinary share capital of CD on 1 January 20X3 for $1,172,000.

The consolidated statement of financial position of the AB Group at 31 December 20X2 reflected a balance on the NCI reserve relating to CD of $3,030,000.

The adjustment that would be made to consolidated reserves as a result of the acquisition of the additional shares in CD on 1 January 20X3 is:

A $162,000 debit
B $162,000 credit
C $869,000 debit
D $869,000 credit

128 ROB acquired a 15% investment in PER on 1 May 20X0 for $600,000. The investment was classified as FVOCI and the gains earned on it have been recorded within other reserves in ROB's individual financial statements. The fair value of the 15% investment at 1 April 20X2 was $800,000.

On 1 April 20X2, ROB acquired an additional 60% of the equity share capital of PER at a cost of $2,900,000. In its own financial statements, ROB has kept its investment in PER as an FVOCI asset recorded at its fair value of $4,000,000 as at the year-end, 30 September 20X2.

It is group policy to value non-controlling interest (NCI) at fair value at the date of acquisition. The fair value of the NCI at 1 April 20X2 was $1.25 million.

Which of the following statements are true in respect of ROB's investment in PER? Select all that apply.

A Goodwill will be calculated at both acquisition dates and the total presented in the consolidated financial statements of ROB

B $200,000 will be reclassified from other comprehensive income to profit or loss on 1 April 20X2

C The goodwill included in the consolidated financial statements will relate solely to the 60% acquisition of PER's shares

D At the reporting date, ROB will have recorded gains of $500,000 in other reserves in its individual financial statements in respect of its investments in PER and this should be reversed out on consolidation

E Goodwill is initially calculated at 1 April 20X2 and will include the fair value of the original 15% holding in PER

129 The PT group acquired 30% of the ordinary share capital of FG for $100,000 a number of years ago. On 1 October 20X5 it acquired a further 40% of the ordinary share capital of FG for $500,000. The group includes a number of other subsidiaries and associates and has a reporting date of 31 December 20X5.

Which one of the following statements in respect of the purchase of the additional shares in FG on 1 October 20X5 is true?

A A gain on disposal of associate will be recognised in the consolidated statement of profit or loss and the results of FG will be consolidated for the final three months only

B Goodwill arising on the acquisition will include consideration paid of $600,000 to reflect the cost of both shareholdings

C The additional 40% is recognised as a transfer between owners and an adjustment is made to PT's reserves to reflect the difference between the consideration paid and change in value of the non-controlling interest

D The consolidated statement of financial position will include an investment in associate to reflect the 30% investment that was held for the majority of the year

130 ZX acquired 40% of the equity share capital of NM for $270 million in 20X0 when the fair value of the net assets of NM was $600 million. ZX exerts significant influence over NM at this point. ZX acquired a further 30% of the equity share capital of NM for $260 million on 1 October 20X3 when the fair value of the net assets was $800 million. The fair value of the initial 40% investment in NM was $390 million at 1 October 20X3.

The gain that would be recorded in the consolidated statement of profit or loss of the ZX Group as a result of the acquisition of the additional shares in NM on 1 October 20X3 is:

A $nil

B $40 million

C $120 million

D $300 million

131 BH acquired 25% of the equity shares of NJ a number of years ago. On 1 June 20X1 BH acquired an additional 30% of the equity shares of NJ.

Which THREE of the following statements are true in respect of the year to 31 December 20X1?

A BH will continue to exercise significant influence over NJ from 1 June 20X1

B BH will calculate goodwill on the acquisition of NJ at 1 June 20X1 as it can now exercise control over NJ

C The 25% existing holding in NJ will be included in the goodwill calculation at its fair value

D Non-controlling interest in NJ will be recognised and included in the equity section of the consolidated statement of financial position as at 31 December 20X1

E The investment in NJ will be equity accounted in the consolidated statement of profit or loss throughout the year ended 31 December 20X1

132 AB acquired a 10% investment in CD on 1 February 20W9 for $800,000. On 1 January 20X2, AB acquired an additional 60% of the equity share capital of CD at a cost of $5,175,000. The fair value of the original 10% investment at 1 January 20X2 was $1,000,000.

The fair value of the net assets of CD on 1 January 20X2 was $6,500,000. It is group policy to value non-controlling interest (NCI) at fair value at the date of acquisition. The fair value of the NCI in CD on 1 January 20X2 was $2,700,000.

The goodwill arising on the acquisition of CD that would be reflected in the consolidated financial statements of the AB group at 1 January 20X2 is:

A $1,375,000

B $1,625,000

C $2,175,000

D $2,375,000

133 HN purchased 30% of the ordinary share capital of ST a number of years ago. On 1 April 20X5, HN purchased a further 45% of the ordinary share capital of ST. An extract from the statements of profit or loss and other comprehensive income of HN and ST for the year ended 31 December 20X5 is below.

Statement of profit or loss and other comprehensive income extract	HN group (excluding ST) $000	ST $000
Profit for the year	500	220
Other comprehensive income	40	25
Total comprehensive income	540	245

At 1 April 20X5, the book value of ST's net assets was considered to be equal to fair value. Goodwill arising on the investment in ST was tested for impairment but none had arisen at the year end.

HN has a number of other wholly owned subsidiaries whose results are already consolidated in the above figures. Comprehensive income is assumed to accrue evenly throughout the year.

The profit attributable to the non-controlling interest in the consolidated statement of profit or loss and other comprehensive income of the HN group for the year ended 31 December 20X5 is:

A $41,250
B $45,938
C $49,500
D $55,000

134 FD acquired 80% of the ordinary share capital of BN a number of years ago and goodwill arising on the acquisition was $200,000. No impairment has been recognised since acquisition. It is group policy to measure non-controlling interest at fair value at the date of acquisition. On 1 September 20X3 FD sold three quarters of its shareholding in BN for $560,000 and the fair value of the remaining holding was $175,000. The balance on the non-controlling interest at 31 August 20X3 was $70,000.

Which THREE of the following statements are true in respect of the preparation of the group financial statements of FD for the year to 31 December 20X3?

A   A gain on disposal of subsidiary should be recognised in the statement of profit or loss
B   The fair value of the remaining holding is the initial measurement of the financial asset that should be recognised from 1 September 20X3
C   The gain on disposal calculation should reflect the sale proceeds of $560,000 netted off against 75% of the carrying amount of the net assets, goodwill and non-controlling interest at the date of disposal
D   The goodwill remaining after disposal is $50,000 (25% of the original carrying amount)
E   The NCI balance will be debited by $52,500
F   The NCI balance will be debited by $70,000

OBJECTIVE TEST QUESTIONS : SECTION 1

135 ST acquired 80% of the 250,000 $1 ordinary shares of UV in 20W8. On 1 October 20X1 ST then disposed of 20,000 of the shares for $115,000.

Which THREE of the following statements are true in respect of the preparation of the group financial statements of ST for the year to 31 December 20X1?

A The consolidated statement of financial position will no longer include 100% of the assets and liabilities of UV

B The consolidated statement of profit or loss will include the results of UV for the full year ended 31 December 20X1

C Goodwill arising on the acquisition of UV will remain in the consolidated statement of financial position as ST continues to control UV

D The consolidated statement of profit or loss will include non-controlling interest only for the first 9 months of the year

E The NCI reserve will be debited to reflect the sale of shares by ST on 1 October 20X1

F The NCI reserve will be credited to reflect the sale of shares by ST on 1 October 20X1

CONSOLIDATED CASH FLOW STATEMENTS

136 Select, from the list below, THREE items that would be included in the 'cash flows from operating activities' section of the consolidated statement of cash flows.

A Acquisition of subsidiary, net of cash acquired

B Disposal of subsidiary, net of cash sold

C Dividends received from associate

D Gain on sale of subsidiary

E Goodwill impairment

F Share of associate profit for the year

137 In a consolidated statement of cash flows, which TWO of the following would be reflected as investing cash flows of the group?

A Dividend received from an associate

B Gain on disposal of an associate

C Acquisition of associate

D Share of associate other comprehensive income

E Share of associate profit or loss

138 DF's consolidated statement of financial position shows inventories with a carrying amount of $34,800,000 at 31 December 20X2 and $36,000,000 at 31 December 20X1.

DF disposed of its entire holding in SD on 1 October 20X2, when the carrying amount of the inventories in SD was $3,600,000.

The adjustment that should be made to profit to reflect the movement in inventories within the operating activities section of the consolidated statement of cash flows of the DF group for the year ended 31 December 20X2 is:

A $2,400,000 deduction

B $2,400,000 addition

C $4,800,000 deduction

D $4,800,000 addition

SUBJECT F2 : ADVANCED FINANCIAL REPORTING

139 MIC's consolidated statement of financial position shows property, plant and equipment with a carrying amount of $16,800,000 at 31 March 20X7 and $15,600,000 at 31 March 20X6.

There were no disposals of property, plant and equipment in the year. Depreciation charged in arriving at profit totalled $1,800,000. MIC disposed of its entire holding in GH on 1 December 20X6 for $4 million. The fair value of the property, plant and equipment in GH at 1 December 20X6 was $800,000.

Calculate the cash outflow from purchase of property, plant and equipment that would appear within the investing activities section of the consolidated statement of cash flows of the MIC Group for the year ended 31 March 20X7.

Give your answer to the nearest $000.

The following scenario relates to questions 140 to 141 (2 questions)

An extract from AB's consolidated statement of financial position at 31 December 20X1 is as follows:

	20X1	20X0
Equity attributable to owners of the parent:	$000	$000
Revaluation reserve	1,250	–
Retained earnings	21,850	20,100
Non-controlling interests	19,500	18,300

An extract from AB's consolidated statement of profit or loss and other comprehensive income for the year ended 31 December 20X1 is as follows:

Profit for the year attributable to:	$000
Owners of the parent	3,880
Non-controlling interests	610
	4,490
Total comprehensive income attributable to:	
Owners of the parent	5,130
Non-controlling interests	680
	5,810

AB acquired 70% of the ordinary share capital of XY on 1 January 20X1 when XY's net assets had a fair value of $4,400,000. The group policy is to value the NCI at acquisition at its proportionate share of the fair value of the net assets. There were no other purchases or sales of investments in the year.

---

140 The dividends paid to the NCI that would appear in the cash flows from financing activities section of the consolidated statement of cash flows of the AB Group for the year ended 30 June 20X1 is:

- A $520,000
- B $730,000
- C $800,000
- D $3,200,000

141 Calculate the dividends paid to the parent shareholders that would appear in the cash flows from financing activities section of the consolidated statement of cash flows of the AB Group for the year ended 30 June 20X1. State your answer to the nearest $000.

142 GH's consolidated statement of financial position shows an investment in associate of $6,200,000 at 30 June 20X2 and $5,700,000 at 30 June 20X1. There were no acquisitions or disposals of associates in the year ended 30 June 20X2.

GH's share of associate profit for the year ended 30 June 20X2 was $1,800,000. The share of associate's other comprehensive income was $200,000.

The dividends received from associate that would appear in the cash flows from investing activities section of the consolidated statement of cash flows of the GH Group for the year ended 30 June 20X2 is:

- A $1,100,000
- B $1,500,000
- C $2,100,000
- D $2,500,000

143 BC's consolidated statement of financial position shows a carrying amount of goodwill of $8 million at 31 May 20X1 and $7.2 million at 31 May 20X0.

BC acquired 70% of the ordinary share capital of YZ on 1 January 20X1 for a cash consideration of $500,000 plus the issue of 1 million $1 ordinary shares in BC, which had a deemed value of $3.95 per share at the date of acquisition. The fair values of the net assets acquired on 1 January 20X1 were $4.4 million.

The group policy is to value the non-controlling interests at acquisition at its proportionate share of the fair value of the net assets.

The goodwill impairment that would be reflected as an adjustment from profit to net cash from operations in the consolidated statement of cash flows of the BC Group for the year ended 31 May 20X1 is:

- A $570,000
- B $750,000
- C $800,000
- D $2,170,000

FOREIGN CURRENCY CONSOLIDATIONS

144 IAS® 21 *The effects of changes in foreign exchange rates* governs the translation of foreign operations.

Which TWO of the following statements are true in respect of foreign subsidiaries and their treatment in consolidated financial statements?

- A Exchange differences arising on the translation of a foreign operation are recognised in the statement of profit or loss
- B Goodwill should be translated in the consolidated statement of financial position at the closing rate
- C Subsidiaries are required to present their financial statements in the presentation currency of the parent
- D The exchange difference arising on translation of goodwill is always allocated between parent shareholders and non-controlling interest
- E The exchange difference arising on translation of net assets is always allocated between parent shareholders and non-controlling interest

145 FG acquired 100% of the ordinary share capital of KL on 1 August 20X4 for 204,000 Crowns. KL's share capital at that date comprised 1,000 ordinary shares of 1 Crown each and its reserves were 180,000 Crowns. The carrying amount of KL's net assets was considered to be the same as fair value.

FG's directors conducted an impairment review of the goodwill at 31 July 20X5 and concluded that goodwill had lost 10% of its value during the year as a result of losses made by the subsidiary.

FG presents its consolidated financial statements in $.

The relevant exchange rates are as follows:

1 August 20X4	$1=1.7 Crowns
31 July 20X5	$1=2.2 Crowns
Average rate for the year ended 31 July 20X5	$1=1.9 Crowns

Calculate the value of goodwill that will be presented in FG's consolidated financial statements at 31 July 20X5 in $ to the nearest whole number.

OBJECTIVE TEST QUESTIONS : SECTION 1

146 A acquired 80% of the equity share capital of B on 1 January 20X1. A's presentational and functional currency is the A$. B presents its financial statements in the B$. It is group policy to value the non-controlling interest at the proportionate share of the fair value of the net assets.

The A group's consolidated statement of profit or loss and other comprehensive income for the year ended 31 December 20X1 includes the following exchange difference arising on the translation of B:

Exchange loss on translation of B	A$000
On goodwill	(100)
On net assets	(50)
Total exchange loss for year	(150)

B's profit for the year was B$800,000 and it had no other comprehensive income.

Relevant exchange rates are as follows:

1 January 20X1	A$1=B$2.00
31 December 20X1	A$1=B$2.30
Average rate for the year ended 31 December 20X1	A$1=B$2.10

The total comprehensive income attributable to the non-controlling interest of B reflected in the consolidated statement of profit or loss and other comprehensive income of the A Group for the year ended 31 December 20X1 to the nearest A$ is:

A A$ 46,190
B A$ 56,190
C A$ 66,190
D A$ 86,290

147 Place the following options into the highlighted boxes in the table below to correctly reflect the calculation of the exchange difference for the year arising on translation of a foreign subsidiary's net assets that would be shown in the consolidated statement of other comprehensive income.

Acquisition rate
Average rate for the year
Closing rate
Opening rate
Less: net assets at acquisition
Less: opening net assets

Exchange difference on net assets		$
Closing net assets at		X
Less: comprehensive income at		(X)
		(X)
Exchange difference on net assets for the year		X

148

Goodwill at acquisition (Crowns 000):
- Consideration: 13,984
- NCI at fair value: 3,496
- Less: FV of net assets: (15,800)
- Goodwill: 1,680

Impairment (20%) = 336 Crowns; Closing goodwill = 1,344 Crowns

Translation ($000):
	Crowns 000	Rate	$000
Goodwill at acquisition	1,680	1.61	1,043
Impairment	(336)	1.58	(213)
	1,344		830
Goodwill at 31 Dec 20X1	1,344	1.52	884
Exchange gain on goodwill			54

Exchange difference on translation of goodwill ≈ **$54,000 gain** (to nearest $000).

149

Opening net assets (31 Dec 20X2) = 3,800 − 1,350 = 2,450 dinar (000)

	Dinar 000	Rate	$000
Opening net assets	2,450	36	68.056
Comprehensive income	1,350	35	38.571
			106.627
Closing net assets	3,800	32	118.750
Exchange gain			12.123

Answer: C $12,123 gain

150 B   A$ 563,380

151 B $13,961,585

152 BH prepares its financial statements in dollars, its functional currency, and is considering acquiring 80% of the equity share capital of NJ.

NJ is based overseas in a country that uses the Kron as its currency. NJ sources all its raw materials locally, recruits a local workforce and is subject to local taxes and corporate regulations. Most of its sales however are to customers in other countries.

If the acquisition goes ahead, NJ will continue to operate relatively autonomously within the group and will raise its own finance locally.

Which of the following statements are true?

Select ALL that apply.

A   NJ will be a subsidiary of BH and should therefore select the dollar as its functional currency because the entities are part of a group

B   The functional currency of NJ will be determined by the currency that dominates the primary economic environment in which NJ operates

C   The functional currency of NJ cannot be the Kron as the majority of the sales revenue is not denominated in this currency

D   NJ should adopt the Kron as its functional currency

E   NJ must adopt the Kron as its presentational currency

ANALYSIS OF FINANCIAL PERFORMANCE AND POSITION

153 The following is an extract from the statement of financial position of KER:

	$ million
Equity:	
Share capital ($1 shares)	100
Revaluation reserve	74
Other reserves	32
Retained earnings	457
Total equity	**663**
Non-current liabilities	
Long-term borrowings	400
Redeemable preference shares	100
Deferred tax	37
Warranty provision	12
Total non-current liabilities	**549**

Giving your answer as a percentage to one decimal place, what is KER's gearing ratio (calculated as debt/equity)?

OBJECTIVE TEST QUESTIONS : SECTION 1

154 Extract from the statement of profit or loss of GD for the year ended 30 June 20X1

	$m
Gross profit	360
Distribution costs	(40)
Administrative expenses	(130)
Finance costs	(11)
Profit before tax	179

Extract from the statement of financial position of GD as at 30 June 20X1

	$m
Non-current liabilities:	
Long-term borrowings	90
Deferred taxation	15
	105

Calculate the interest cover for GD for the year to 30 June 20X1.

Give your answer to one decimal place.

155 Extract from the statement of profit or loss of SDF for the year ended 31 October 20X1

	$m
Gross profit	268
Operating expenses	(55)
Share of profit of associate	37
Finance costs	(12)
Profit before tax	238

Extract from the statement of financial position of SDF as at 31 October 20X1

	$m
Non-current assets:	
Property, plant and equipment	381
Investment in associate	86
	467
Equity:	
Share capital	200
Retained reserves	265
Total equity	465
Non-current liabilities:	
Long-term borrowings	190
Deferred tax	25

Calculate the return on capital employed of SDF for the year to 31 October 20X1, excluding the impact of the associate from your calculation.

Give your answer as a percentage to one decimal place.

156 The Return on Capital Employed (ROCE) for DF has increased from 12.3% to 17.8% in the year to 31 March 20X5.

Which one of the following independent options would be a valid reason for this increase?

A   Significant investment in property, plant and equipment shortly before the year end

B   Revaluation of land and buildings following a change of policy from cost model to revaluation model

C   Property, plant and equipment acquired in the previous period now operating at full capacity

D   An issue of equity shares with the proceeds being used to repay long-term borrowings

157 The following is an extract from the financial statements of ST for the year to 31 December 20X3:

Equity and liabilities	20X3 $m	20X2 $m
Share capital	400	250
Share premium	200	50
Revaluation reserve	158	35
Retained earnings	350	470
Total equity	1,108	805
Non-current liabilities		
Long-term borrowings	530	480

Which THREE of the following statements about the changes in the capital structure of ST could be realistically concluded from the extract provided above?

A   ST must have made a loss in the year as retained earnings have fallen

B   A revaluation surplus in the year has contributed to the reduction in gearing

C   Shares were issued at a premium to nominal value

D   ST may have paid a significant dividend in the year

E   ST must have secured additional long-term borrowings of $50m

OBJECTIVE TEST QUESTIONS : SECTION 1

158 An investor is considering two potential investments, A and B, and extracts from the entities' statements of financial position are below:

	A	B
	$000	$000
Total equity	3,754	3,403
Non-current liabilities:		
5% loan notes	1,000	200
Current liabilities:		
Short-term borrowings	50	80

Entity B's gearing ratio has been calculated to be 5.9%.

The gearing ratio of A that would be comparable with B's ratio above (to the nearest decimal place) is:

- A   21.0%
- B   21.9%
- C   26.6%
- D   28.0%

The following scenario relates to questions 159 to 161 (3 questions)

LOP operates in the construction industry, is listed on its local stock exchange and prepares its financial statements in accordance with IFRS standards. It is looking to expand overseas by acquiring a new subsidiary. Two geographical areas have been targeted, Frontland and Sideland. Entity A operates in Frontland and entity B operates in Sideland. Both entities are listed on their local exchanges.

The financial highlights for entities A, B and LOP are provided below for the last trading period.

	A	B	LOP
Revenue	$160m	$300m	$500m
Gross profit margin	26%	17%	28%
Profit from operations margin	9%	11%	16%
Gearing	65%	30%	38%
Average rate of interest available in the last 12 months	5%	9%	8%

159 Which one of the following statements is a realistic conclusion that could be drawn from the above information?

- A   A appears to be benefiting from economies of scale
- B   B has lower operating expenses than A
- C   A has attracted a lower rate of interest on its borrowings than B because it's gearing level would suggest that is a lower risk to lenders than B
- D   Acquisition of either entity would lead to an improvement in LOP's gross margin due to the increased revenue that would be achieved

SUBJECT F2 : ADVANCED FINANCIAL REPORTING

160 Which of the following statements is true, based on the information provided?

- A A would be a riskier investment than B because it has higher gearing
- B A would give LOP greater benefit in terms of additional borrowing capacity
- C A's high gross profit margin and low operating profit margin proves that the directors of A are partaking in creative accounting
- D A's lower profit from operations margin suggests A operates in the budget sector of the construction market compared to B and LOP

161 Which one of the following statements concerning the use of ratio analysis to make a decision about investing in X or Y is false?

- A A and B may use different accounting standards when preparing their financial statements and this would reduce the comparability of their profit margins
- B A and B may be subject to different tax rates which would reduce the comparability of their profit from operations margins
- C A and B may apply different accounting policies, such as cost model v revaluation model for property, plant and equipment. This would reduce comparability of their gearing ratios
- D Figures could be distorted due to large transactions prior to the year-end

162 RT is seeking expansion by pursuing new markets with its existing product base. The following is an extract from the statement of profit or loss of RT:

	20X9 $m	20X8 $m
Revenue	1,430	1,022
Cost of sales	(1,058)	(705)
Gross profit	372	317
Administrative expenses	(74)	(62)
Distribution costs	(168)	(100)
Profit from operations	130	155

Which one of the following statements could NOT be realistically concluded from the extract provided above?

- A RT may have increased their sales volumes, and therefore revenue, by reducing their selling prices
- B RT's distribution costs have increased in line with the increase in revenue and the main reason for the fall in operating profit margin is the increase in administrative expenses, which should remain relatively fixed
- C The significant increase in distribution costs suggests that RT is supplying goods to new customers that are geographically further away
- D RT's increase in revenue has been achieved at the expense of profit margins

OBJECTIVE TEST QUESTIONS : SECTION 1

163 The following information is available for 2 potential acquisition targets. The entities are situated in the same country and both operate in the same industry.

	A	B
Revenue	$375m	$380m
Gross profit margin	28%	19%
Profit for the year/revenue margin	11%	11%

Which one of the following statements is NOT a valid conclusion that could be drawn from comparing the above information for A and B?

- A A's gross profit margin is better than B's as it is able to benefit from economies of scale
- B The difference between the gross profit margin of A and B may be due to how they classify their expenses between cost of sales and operating costs
- C A may have improved their gross profit margin by significant investment in new and efficient machinery, but could be suffering from high finance costs as a result of financing the investment with long-term borrowings
- D B may be selling a significantly higher volume of products than A but at a lower price

164 Your friend is considering acquiring a small shareholding in AD, an entity listed on the stock market, as she believes that the entity has a promising future. However, having performed some limited analysis on the most recent financial statements of AD she is concerned by some of her findings. Profitability has reduced in the most recent financial period due to a significant increase in administrative expenses. The return on capital employed has fallen, partly due to the increase in expenses but also from a significant investment in property, plant and equipment close to the year end.

The financial statements reviewed by your friend were for the year ended 30 September 20X1. It is now June 20X2.

Which THREE of the following options would be considered realistic next steps for your friend to take prior to investing?

- A Request an analysis of administrative expenses from the entity to understand why they have risen significantly
- B Access articles from the financial press and obtain industry ratio averages and compare performance of AD with other entities in the sector
- C Contact the Chief Financial Officer to ask what is being done to improve profitability and whether the increase in administrative expenses is a one-off event
- D Review the narrative reports within the financial statements that give details of recent investment to assess if the business is undergoing expansion and likely to bring additional future returns
- E Obtain a copy of any interim financial statements published since the previous year end to assess whether performance of the entity has improved

SUBJECT F2 : ADVANCED FINANCIAL REPORTING

165 KL operates in the fashion wholesale business and its management team has become increasingly concerned about the liquidity of the entity. It has asked you for your opinion and you have calculated the following ratios to help you with your assessment:

	30 June 20X3	30 June 20X2
Inventory holding period	128 days	77 days
Receivables collection period	88 days	87 days
Payables payment period	170 days	118 days
Current ratio	1.3:1	2.1:1
Quick ratio	0.7:1	1.4:1

Which one of the following is NOT a valid statement about the ratios shown above?

A   The increase in inventory holding period is a significant concern as there is a high risk of obsolescence in the industry

B   The deterioration in the ratios shown at the 30 June 20X3 year end could simply be a result of a significant purchase of goods being made on credit terms close to the year end

C   KL are attempting to finance their increased inventory holding period by delaying payments to suppliers

D   The significant increase in payables payment period will have caused the cash position to worsen dramatically

166 The following is an extract from the statement of cash flows for QW for the year ended 31 December 20X1:

	$m
Cash flows from operating activities	750
Cash flows from investing activities	(1,130)
Cash flows from financing activities	320
Net cash flow for the year	(60)
Cash and cash equivalents at start of year	650
Cash and cash equivalents at end of year	590

Based on the information provided, which one of the following independent statements would be a reasonable conclusion about the financial adaptability of QW for the year to 31 December 20X1?

A   QW is in decline as there is a significant cash outflow in investing activities

B   QW has financed a high proportion of its investing activities by utilising its operating cash

C   QW must have made a profit in the year, as it has a net cash inflow from operating activities

D   QW must be facing serious liquidity problems as its cash and cash equivalents have fallen by $60 million throughout the year

167 The following is an extract from the financial statements of EE for the year to 31 December 20X1:

Equity and liabilities	20X1 $m	20X0 $m
Share capital	325	195
Share premium	442	364
Revaluation reserve	455	293
Retained earnings	371	585
Total equity	**1,593**	**1,437**
Non-current liabilities		
Long-term borrowings	585	553

Which of the following statements about the changes in the capital structure of EE is a valid conclusion when reviewing the extract provided above?

A EE must have made a loss in the year as retained earnings have fallen

B A revaluation surplus in the year has contributed to a reduction in gearing

C Bonus issues were the only share issues during the year and caused the increase in share capital

D EE must have secured additional long-term borrowings of $25m

168 BH is analysing the financial statements of two potential acquisition targets, VB and JK. VB and JK are of a similar size and operate in the same industry. The gearing of each entity is as follows:

	VB	JK
Gearing	54.3%	31.7%

Which TWO of the following statements could realistically explain the significant difference between the two entities' gearing ratio shown above?

A VB has recorded significant gains on the change in fair value of its FVOCI investments

B VB's management is better at controlling costs than JK's

C VB uses the cost model for property, plant and equipment whereas JK uses the revaluation model

D VB has reduced its effective tax rate by employing tax accountants

E VB relies more on debt finance, whereas JK relies on equity finance

169 ABC is a small private entity looking for investment. It has been trading for more than 10 years manufacturing and selling its own branded perfumes, lotions and candles to the public in its 15 retail stores and to other larger retailing entities. Revenue and profits have been steady over the last 10 years however about 15 months ago ABC set up an online shop and also secured a lucrative deal with a boutique hotel chain to supply products carrying the hotel name and logo.

Extracts from the statement of profit or loss of ABC are provided below:

	20X2 $000	20X1 $000
Revenue	6,000	3,700
Gross profit	1,917	1,095
Profit before tax	540	307

The revenue and profits of the three business segments for the year ended 31 December 20X2 were:

	Retail operations $000	Online store $000	Hotel contract $000
Revenue	4,004	1,096	900
Gross profit	1,200	330	387
Profit before tax	320	138	82

The online store and hotel contract earned a negligible amount of revenue and profit in the year ended 31 December 20X1.

Which THREE of the following statements about the performance of ABC in the year ended 31 December 20X2 could be realistically concluded from the extracts provided above?

A The revenue growth is principally due to the online store and hotel contract

B The gross profit margin would have fallen in 20X2 if the new operations had not been introduced

C The online store should have a better gross profit margin than retail operations as it does not have the shop overheads

D The hotel contract attracts a higher gross profit margin than the other operations

E The hotel contract appears to require significant overheads in comparison to revenue when compared with the other segments

F The increase in profit before tax margin is principally due to the hotel contract

170 CB had 3,750,000 $1 ordinary shares in issue at 1 February 20X4 and did not issue any new shares throughout the year ended 31 January 20X5. It reported a profit for the year ended 31 January 20X5 of $750,000. Dividends of 50c per share were paid during the year.

Calculate the dividend cover for CB at 31 January 20X5.

Give your answer to two decimal places.

OBJECTIVE TEST QUESTIONS : SECTION 1

171 RT is analysing the financial statements of two potential acquisition targets, X and Y, that are of a similar size. The non-current asset turnovers of the two entities are as follows:

	A	B
Non-current asset turnover	3.6	1.1

Which THREE of the following statements could realistically explain the significant difference between the two entities' non-current asset turnover shown above?

- A A's non-current assets are operating more efficiently than B's
- B B has invested in new non-current assets close to the year end
- C A has revalued its non-current assets during the year
- D A operates in a manufacturing industry and B in a service industry
- E A's non-current assets are significantly older than B's

172 Which THREE of the following statements are considered to be benefits to users of segmental analysis disclosures prepared in accordance with IFRS® 8 *Operating Segments* when analysing performance and position of an entity?

- A The disclosures reflect the information used by the chief operating decision maker when making economic decisions about the entity, therefore users get an 'inside view' of management accounting information
- B Users can see how each separate major component of the business is contributing to the overall performance of the entity
- C Entities (in particular) directors have a certain amount of flexibility in how they define the reportable segments
- D Users will be able to compare different entities on a segment by segment basis, rather than just on overall results/position
- E Users may be able to better assess the level of risk facing the entity as each segment will be exposed to different risks

173 DF has an employee share option scheme that vested at the end of the previous financial period. Employees are expected to exercise their options in the next 12 months. Assume that no further equity will be issued by DF in the year.

Which one of the following statements is true if all of the employees whose options vest choose to exercise their options in the current period?

Select ALL that apply.

- A Earnings per share will increase
- B Share prices of DF will remain constant
- C Profit before tax will increase
- D Gearing will decrease

174 Place the following options into the highlighted boxes in the table below to correctly reflect the formulae used to calculate dividend cover.

Net profit for the year
Share price
Dividend per share
Dividend paid during the year
Number of ordinary shares issued

Dividend cover
───────

175 SJ bought an item of plant and machinery for $150,000 on 31 March 20X6, and financed the purchase by taking out a bank loan. The year end is 31 March 20X6.

Which of the following statements are false?

A   SJ's current ratio would remain unaffected by the transaction

B   SJ's gearing would increase due to the increase in debt as at the year end.

C   Interest cover would decrease due to the increased finance costs incurred during the year ended 31st Mar 20X6.

D   ROCE would be expected to reduce as operating profits would be unaffected and capital employed would increase

176 XZ has changed its accounting policy in the year and now revalues all of its non-depreciable land.

Which THREE of the following ratios would be directly affected by this change in policy resulting in a lack of comparability of this year's ratio to that calculated last year?

A   Non-current asset turnover
B   Profit before tax margin
C   Return on capital employed
D   Gearing
E   Current ratio

OBJECTIVE TEST QUESTIONS : SECTION 1

The following scenario relates to questions 177 to 179 (3 questions)

The directors of EMS have recently submitted a loan application for $100 million to finance expansion and have attached their most recent financial statements in support of the application.

Financial highlights from the financial statements are as follows:

	20X2	20X1
Revenue	$2,400m	$2,020m
Gross profit margin	27.7%	25.5%
Profit before tax margin	12.8%	9.2%
Return on capital employed	15.5%	16.1%

Extracts from statement of financial position as at 31 December:

	20X2 $m	20X1 $m
Assets		
Property, plant and equipment	766	448
Cash and cash equivalents	–	144
Equity		
Share capital	300	300
Revaluation reserve	155	70
Other reserves	44	44
Retained earnings	801	633
Total equity	1,300	1,047
Borrowings		
Long-term – 5% convertible bonds 20X4	200	188
Short-term	58	–
	258	188

177 Which one of the following statements provides a valid and reasonable explanation for the reduction in return on capital employed?

    A   Additional long-term borrowings taken out

    B   Increased finance cost from short-term borrowings

    C   Reduction in profit from operations margin

    D   Revaluation of property, plant and equipment

178 Calculate the asset turnover (based on capital employed) for the year ended 31 December 20X2, including both long-term and short-term borrowings. State your answer to two decimal places.

179 Which one of the following is an inappropriate statement regarding the limitations of using the above financial information when making a decision about whether to provide finance to EMS?
- A Different accounting policies can affect comparison of one period to the next
- B Limited extracts provided from the statement of financial position so unable to assess how well EMS manages its working capital
- C Limited extracts provided from statement of profit or loss so unable to see the reason for the improvement in profit before tax margin
- D No industry averages available so cannot see whether improvement is in line with, or exceeds, expectations

180 **Extract from the statements of profit or loss of A and B for the year ended 31 December 20X1**

	A	B
	$000	$000
Gross profit	1,100	1,580
Distribution costs	(375)	(420)
Administrative expenses	(168)	(644)
Share of associate profit	148	25
Finance costs	(25)	(32)
Profit before tax	680	509

Extract from the statements of financial position of A and B as at 31 December 20X1

	$000	$000
Investment in associate	570	350
Total equity	950	1,500
Non-current liabilities (borrowings)	500	650

The return on capital employed of B has been calculated as 28.7%.

The return on capital employed of A that would be comparable to this on a like for like basis is:
- A 38.4%
- B 46.9%
- C 48.6%
- D 63.3%

181 Complete the following sentences by placing one of the options identified below in each of the spaces. The options may be used more than once.

| an increase | a reduction |

When assessing reasons for changes in cash and cash equivalents _____ in inventory, _____ in receivables and _____ in payables would all explain an improvement in the cash position.

OBJECTIVE TEST QUESTIONS : SECTION 1

The following scenario relates to questions 182 to 183 (2 questions)

RB is considering investing in LW, a listed entity that operates in the manufacturing sector. LW operates in a mature market and has not experienced growth in volume for the past five years. It is currently considering ways that it can increase revenue by diversifying its product range however it has yet to implement any new strategy.

The following ratios have been calculated based on LW's most recent financial statements for the year ended 31 December 20X3.

	20X3	20X2
Gross profit margin	39.4%	36.6%
Operating profit margin	12.6%	14.4%
Quick ratio	0.5	1.1
Inventories holding period	141 days	112 days
Payables payment period	154 days	98 days

LW was involved in a major dispute with one of its key customers in 20X3 regarding the non-settlement of amounts owed by the customer. The dispute was eventually settled close to the reporting date and the majority of the cash has since been received, however LW incurred significant legal fees in the process and had to stop supplying the customer for a period of time.

182 Which THREE of the following statements are realistic conclusions that could be drawn from the above ratios and information?

    A   Stopping supplies to the significant customer will have contributed to the increase in inventory holding period

    B   The impact of the cost of the dispute can be seen in the operating profit margin, which has fallen despite an increase in gross profit margin for the year

    C   The increase in gross profit margin is likely to have been achieved by increasing selling prices

    D   The increase in payables payment period will have resulted in a reduction in cash and cash equivalents

    E   The reduction in quick ratio is principally due to the significant increase in inventory holding period

    F   The reduction in quick ratio is principally due to the significant increase in payables payment period

183 Which of the following would NOT be readily available to help RB decide whether to invest in LW?

Select ALL that apply.

    A   Breakdown of operating expenses to establish reasons for fall in operating margin

    B   Cash flow forecasts to assess likely post year end liquidity

    C   Industry average statistics to compare performance with other entities in the sector

    D   Interim financial information that may have been published since the 20X3 year end

    E   Operating and financial review (management commentary)

SUBJECT F2 : ADVANCED FINANCIAL REPORTING

184 Place the following options into the highlighted boxes in the table below to correctly reflect the formulae used to calculate both return on capital employed and gross profit margin. The same option may be used more than once.

Revenue
Revenue – cost of sales
Equity
Revenue – cost of sales – operating expenses
Non-current assets
Capital employed

Return on capital employed	Gross profit margin
———————	———————

185 Which one of the following statements is NOT a limitation of comparing ratios of two entities listed on stock exchanges in different countries?

- A If entities are located in different geographical markets they may be exposed to different economic pressures and variables such as interest rates and tax rates which will distort any comparison of earnings per share
- B The dividend cover will be incomparable as share prices may be affected by differing levels of liquidity in their respective markets
- C The financial statements of the entities could be prepared using different accounting standards, resulting in incomparable earnings per share
- D The companies can use different calculations to determine the same ratio.

186 Which of the following would be readily available information to a minority shareholder of a listed entity?

Select ALL that apply.

- A Cash flow forecasts for the next five years
- B Share price information
- C Operating and financial review/management commentary
- D Trend analysis (results over period of time)
- E Analysis of expenses
- F Size of order book (to assess future prospects)

OBJECTIVE TEST QUESTIONS : SECTION 1

The following scenario relates to questions 187 to 189 (3 questions)

ABC prepares its financial statements in accordance with International Financial Reporting Standards and is listed on its local stock exchange. ABC is considering the acquisition of overseas operations. Two geographical areas have been targeted, X-land and Y-land. Entity X operates in X-land and entity Y operates in Y-land.

The most recent financial statements of entities X and Y have been converted into ABC's currency for ease of comparison. The financial indicators from these financial statements are provided below.

	X	Y
Revenue	$390m	$400m
Gross profit margin	28%	19%
Profit after tax/revenue × 100	10%	11%
Gearing	66%	26%
Average rate of interest available in the respective markets	5%	10%

187 Which one of the following statements is NOT a valid potential explanation of the difference in gross profit margins reflected above?

    A   X and Y do not operate in the same industry

    B   X and Y sell the same products but have a different sales/product mix

    C   X classifies certain expenses as cost of sales that Y classifies as operating expenses

    D   X sells lower volume but higher quality products than Y

188 Which one of the following statements would NOT be a valid explanation of the difference in gearing ratios reflected above?

    A   X has recently replaced its plant and equipment and Y is yet to do so

    B   X revalues its non-current assets whereas Y uses the cost model

    C   X wishes to limit its voting rights to a small number of shareholders

    D   X wishes to take advantage of relatively cheap debt finance

189 Complete the following sentences by placing one of the options identified below in each of the spaces.

X	Y	ABC
less	more	

If further debt finance was required by the new companies, debt finance would be _____ likely to be obtained for Y.

Based upon the gearing levels of the two entities, an investment in _____ would appear to be riskier than an investment in _____.

190 The following information is available for entity SAF:

Six month period ended:	31 Dec 20X2	30 Jun 20X2
Revenue	$3.1m	$2m
Gross profit margin	21.9%	27.5%
Current ratio	2.0	2.4
Quick ratio	1.2	1.6
Inventories holding period	92 days	58 days
Receivables collection period	101 days	72 days
Payables payment period	90 days	73 days

Which TWO of the following statements about SAF could NOT be realistically concluded from the above financial information?

A SAF is facing serious liquidity problems

B The increase in inventories holding period may be in response to the extra demand for products reflected in the increased revenue

C The reduction in quick ratio is caused by the increase in inventory holding period

D The significant expansion in revenue is likely to have been achieved by reducing selling prices

E There are signs of over-trading

191 Which one of the following statements correctly identifies the effect that an upwards revaluation of non-current assets would have on return on capital employed (ROCE) and gearing?

A Increase in both ROCE and gearing

B Decrease in both ROCE and gearing

C Increase in ROCE and decrease in gearing

D Decrease in ROCE and increase in gearing

192 Which of the following would be accessible information for a potential lender of a significant level of finance?

Select ALL that apply.

A Cash flow forecasts for the next five years

B Information about existing finance arrangements

C Operating and financial review/management commentary

D Trend analysis (results over period of time)

E Detailed analysis of expenses

F Size of order book (to assess future prospects)

OBJECTIVE TEST QUESTIONS : SECTION 1

The following scenario relates to questions 193 to 194 (2 questions)

XZ is seeking to grow through acquisition and has identified two unlisted entities, A and B, of similar size and operating in the same line of business and in the same country, as potential acquisition targets. A and B have similar levels of capital employed, but the balance between equity and debt differs.

Extracts from the most recent financial statements are:

Statement of profit or loss and other comprehensive income	A	B
	$000	$000
Revenue	5,700	5,300
Finance costs	(120)	(105)
Other comprehensive income:		
Revaluation surplus	200	–

The following key financial ratios have been calculated to assist with the investment decision.

	A	B
Gross profit margin	36.0%	31.0%
Profit before tax margin	11.5%	14.0%
Return on capital employed	27.4%	22.2%
Gearing (at the year-end)	34.3%	55.2%

193 Complete the following sentences by placing one of the options identified below in each of the spaces.

higher	because of
lower	despite

A is incurring significantly _____ operating expenses than B. Its return on capital employed is higher than B's _____ the revaluation of non-current assets in the year.

194 Which one of the following statements would NOT be a valid explanation for the difference in gearing and finance costs between A and B?

A   A has a revaluation policy for its non-current assets whereas B adopts the cost model

B   B distributes more of its profits to its shareholders in dividend payments

C   A pays a higher rate of interest on its borrowings

D   If the rate of interest on borrowings is similar for both entities, then either A has increased its borrowings or B has repaid a significant amount of borrowings part way through the year

SUBJECT F2 : ADVANCED FINANCIAL REPORTING

195 A Ltd has purchased its computer equipment using debt finance, whereas B Ltd leases computer equipment under a lease agreement. The leases were deemed low value leases. Both entities use their computer equipment for administrative purposes.

Which of the following ratios would be considered incomparable between the two entities based on the way the entities have financed their purchases of computer equipment?

Select ALL that apply.

A   Gross profit margin
B   Non-current asset turnover
C   Return on capital employed
D   Current ratio
E   Gearing
F   Interest cover

196 The following is an extract from the financial statements of WX for the year to 31 December 20X5:

Equity and liabilities	20X5 $m	20X4 $m
Share capital	500	400
Share premium	300	400
Revaluation reserve	340	–
Retained earnings	300	470
Total equity	**1,440**	**1,270**
Non-current liabilities		
Long-term borrowings	360	320

Which one of the following statements about the changes in the capital structure of WX is a valid conclusion that can be drawn from the extract provided above?

A   WX must have made a loss in the year
B   WX may have adopted the revaluation policy to offset a significant loss in the year and maintain the gearing level
C   WX has raised finance via a share issue
D   WX must have taken out additional borrowings of $40 million

197 Complete the following sentences by placing one of the options identified below in each of the spaces. The options may be used more than once.

| operating | investing | financing |

When analysing a statement of cash flows, a cash outflow from _____ activities would suggest that the entity is expanding its operations.

An outflow from investing activities is often matched with an inflow from _____ activities as long term finance should be used to finance investment.

OBJECTIVE TEST QUESTIONS : SECTION 1

The following scenario relates to questions 198 to 200 (3 questions)

TYU is a listed entity that operates in a highly competitive market. A new entrant to this market has created pressure amongst the competitive entities by developing a marginally lower quality product and selling it at a lower price. The result has been a shift in market share to this new entrant in the last few months of the financial period just ended.

Extracts from TYU's financial information for the year are as follows:

	20X2	20X1
	$	$
Revenue	$678m	$618m
Gross profit margin	32.4%	35.0%
Operating profit margin	5.2%	4.6%
Current ratio	1.3	2.0
Quick ratio	0.5	1.1
Inventories holding period	167 days	100 days
Receivables collection period	65 days	60 days
Payables payment period	156 days	109 days
Cash and cash equivalents	–	$24m
Short-term borrowings	$47m	–

198 Complete the following sentences by placing one of the options identified below in each of the spaces.

| a reduction in selling prices | an increase in cost of sales per unit |

Given the circumstances that TYU finds itself in, the most likely reason for the reduction in gross profit margin is _____.

199 Which one of the following statements is a valid conclusion that can be drawn from the above ratios?

A   The increase in inventory holding period has resulted in a fall in current ratio

B   The increase in inventory holding period has resulted in a fall in quick ratio

C   The increase in the inventory holding period has resulted in a reduction in cash

D   The increase in inventory holding period has resulted in a fall in gross profit margin

200 Which one of the following statements is NOT a valid conclusion that can be drawn from the above ratios?

A   As the current ratio is greater than 1 there are no major liquidity concerns

B   The increase in payables payment period has been caused by the lack of cash

C   The increase in receivables collection period has contributed to the lack of cash

D   The management of TYU have controlled costs well to minimise the impact of the new entrant on profit

SUBJECT F2 : ADVANCED FINANCIAL REPORTING

201 Which of the following differences in accounting policies between two entities could affect the comparison of their gross profit margins?

Select ALL that apply.

- A Different depreciation rates on plant and equipment
- B First-in-first-out versus average cost method for valuing inventory
- C Method for valuing non-controlling interest at the date of acquisition of a subsidiary
- D Revaluation of non-current assets versus cost model
- E Different classification of costs between cost of sales and operating expenses
- F Input (cost) basis versus output (work certified) basis for calculating stage of completion of a contract with a customer which recognises revenue over time

202 Below are extracts from the statement of profit or loss and other comprehensive income of JS Inc for the year ended 31 Oct 20X5:

	$000
Gross profit	430
Distribution costs	(32)
Administrative expenses	(159)
Operating Profit	239
Finance costs	(15)
Profit before tax	224

Included within administrative expenses was $15,000 of depreciation, $23,000 salaries to staff and $12,000 amortisation of intangible assets.

Included within distribution expenses are $5,000 of depreciation and $8,000 fuel costs.

EBITDA for JS Inc for the year ended 31st Oct 20X5 is (quoted in $000's):

- A 146
- B 177
- C 271
- D 302

RANDOM QUESTION TESTS

RANDOM QUESTION TEST 1

1.1 Which of the following statements are false in relation to IFRS 2 *Share-based payments*?

   A   Share-based payments can be used to generate loyalty with staff members by allocating vesting conditions linked to a period of minimum employment.

   B   Share-based payments used to pay staff lead to an expense in the profit or loss. This expense represents the cost to the entity of the services provided by the employee over the vesting period.

   C   Share-based payments will create an equity balance on the statement of financial position.

   D   Share-based payments can be used to pay suppliers as well as employees.

1.2 AB issued 30,000 5% $100 bonds on 1 January 20X1 at par value, incurring issue costs of $25,000. The bonds will be redeemed after five years at a premium of 10%. Which one of the following statements is correct?

   A   The bonds are classified as an amortised cost financial asset

   B   The effective rate of interest on the bonds is greater than 5%

   C   The initial recognition of the bonds will be at a value of $3,025,000

   D   The carrying amount of the bond at each year end will always be $3,300,000

1.3 PF Ltd has issued irredeemable 12% bonds with a market value of $91. The cost of debt is 9.76%.

   What is the tax rate used in PF's jurisdiction to the nearest %?

1.4 TUS has an 80% subsidiary, WXV. WXV, which has been a subsidiary of TUS for the whole year, reported a profit after tax of $600,000 in its own financial statements. You ascertain the following additional matters:

   At the year-end there was unrealised profit of $60,000 on sales by WXV to TUS.

   During the year the goodwill on acquisition of WXV was impaired by $50,000.

   TUS measures the non-controlling interest in WXV using the fair value method.

   What is the non-controlling interest in WXV that would be reported in the consolidated statement of profit or loss and other comprehensive income of TUS for the year?

   A $98,000
   B $108,000
   C $110,000
   D $120,000

SUBJECT F2 : ADVANCED FINANCIAL REPORTING

1.5 The following extracts of the financial statements of Couts Ltd have been obtained:

	20X5
Inventories	$195,000
Receivables	$120,000
Cash	$15,000
Loan repayable 20X8	$135,000
Deferred tax	$21,000
Payables	$105,000
Overdraft	$51,000

What is the quick ratio of Couts Ltd?

A   0.76:1
B   0.87:1
C   1.86:1
D   2.12:1

1.6 Which of the following is not a valid reason for an increase in the level of gearing?

A   A revaluation loss has been recorded in the year
B   New shares were issued during the year
C   A new loan has been taken out in the year
D   New high value assets were acquired under leases during the year

1.7 EMI owns 75% of the 1m ordinary shares of LI. EMI's holding in LI was acquired on 31st July 20X9 with a cost of $10m. LI paid $4m to acquire 65% of A on the 31st December 20X8.

Which of the following statements are correct? Select all that apply.

A   Goodwill of A will include an indirect holding adjustment of $1m
B   The goodwill of A will include the fair value of the net assets of A as at the 31st Dec 20X8
C   Goodwill of Li will include an indirect holding adjustment of $2.5m
D   EMI group retained earnings will include 75% of Li's post acquisition profits
E   EMI group retained earnings will include 65% of A's post acquisition profits

OBJECTIVE TEST QUESTIONS : SECTION 1

1.8 BET is a construction company. They have entered into a contract with HPY to build a large theme park on land owned by HPY. The job was expected to take 4 years to complete. The contract price was agreed at $12m. The contract was expected to make a profit.

BET uses the work certified basis to determine the stage of completion. By the end of the 2nd year, a surveyor considered the contract to be 65% complete. $3.25m revenue was recorded during year 1.

What amount of revenue will be recorded within the statement of profit or loss for year 2?

- A $3.25m
- B $4.55m
- C $7.80m
- D $12m

1.9 SHA owns 70% of RAT. SHA regularly purchases goods from RAT. On the 28th November 20X1, RAT despatched goods with a selling value of $2.5m to SHA. The goods were not delivered to SHA until 5th December 20X1. At the year-ended 30th November 20X1, SHA's statement of financial position showed a trade payable owed to RAT of $45m.

What is the impact of the adjustment that will be required to reflect this information within the consolidated statement of financial position for the SHA group?

- A Inventory increases by $2.5m
  Receivables decreases by $45m
  Payables decreases by $45m
- B Inventory decreases by $2.5m
  Receivables decreases by $45m
  Payables decreases by 45m
- C Inventory increases by $2.5m
  Receivables decreases by $45m
  Payables decreases by $47.5m
- D Inventory increases by $2.5m
  Receivables decreases by $47.5m
  Payables decreases by $45m

1.10 Y and Z operate in a similar industry. Y has payables days of 35 days. Z has payables days of 88 days. Both entities buy goods on 60 day payment terms and offer customers 30 day payment terms. No settlement discounts are available to or offered by the entities.

Which of the following statements are reasonable? Choose all that apply.

A   Analysis should be made of Z's liquidity to assess whether its long payable days indicate cash flow problems.

B   Company Y is operating efficiently and managing their cash balances as effectively as possible by paying suppliers on time.

C   Both companies have negotiated well with suppliers to obtain credit terms which are longer than the credit terms the companies offer to their customers.

D   Company Z's direc5/tors are displaying good management by retaining cash for longer as it is a cheap source of finance.

E   Company Y requires an overdraft to finance its business model.

F   Company Z is at risk of stock outs if suppliers refuse to continue to sell on credit.

RANDOM QUESTION TEST 2

2.1 Suarez Ltd's financial statements for the year ended 31st December 20X5 include a provision of $1m in relation to a court case. Suarez is being sued as an employee was injured as a result of an "incident" involving the chief executive after an important client tender had been lost. The court case has been contested for a long period of time and the carrying amount of the provision at 31st December 20X4 was $500,000.

The provision will not be considered for tax purposes until any damages are paid. The tax rate in the jurisdiction in which Suarez Ltd is operational is 25%.

Which of the following statements is true?

A   The deferred tax liability as at the year-end will have a value of $250,000

B   A charge to reserves of $125k will be recorded during the year ended 31st December 20X5

C   A debit to the deferred tax balance on the statement of financial position is required

D   The temporary difference between carrying amount and tax base as at the year ended 31st December 20X5 is $500,000

2.2 Which ONE of the following statements is a characteristic of ordinary shares?

A   The dividend payment is a fixed proportion of the nominal value of the shares

B   Upon liquidation of a company, the shareholders will receive a pay-out after all other finance providers have been paid

C   Dividends are treated as a finance cost and are paid out of pre-tax profits

D   The shareholders don't have any right to vote on key matters

2.3 Gerrard's financial statements for the year ended 31st December 20X5 show a profit for the year of $3.4million. On 1 January, Gerrard had 4 million shares in issue. On 1 April, 1 million new shares were issued at the full market price.

Gerrard also have $2.5 million 5% convertible loan stock in issue, which can be converted this year into 40 shares for every $100. Gerrard pays tax at 26%. The carrying amount of the liability element of the convertible loan stock is $2million. The effective interest rate is 8%.

What are Gerrard's basic and diluted earnings per share for the year ended 31st December 20X5?

	Basic earnings per share	Diluted earnings per share
A	71.6 cents	61.2 cents
B	71.6 cents	60.7 cents
C	68 cents	58.2 cents
D	68 cents	58.6 cents

2.4 Which of the following items is unlikely to be considered a 'one-off' item which would impact the comparability of ratios?

- A A new website selling direct to the public has meant that deliveries are now made to more diverse geographical areas, increasing delivery costs
- B A closure of a department has led to redundancies
- C Sale of surplus property leading to a profit on disposal
- D A storm in the year led to significant damage to the warehouse

2.5 SJ acquired 60% of the ordinary share capital of DP on 1st January 20X4 for $4,650,000. SJ then purchased a further 20% of the ordinary shares of DP on 1st January 20X5 for $937,500. The NCI balance for DP as at the 31st December 20X4 is $1,860,000.

What will be the adjustment made to consolidated reserves as a result of the acquisition of the additional shares?

- A $7,500 debit
- B $7,500 credit
- C $937,500 debit
- D $937,500 credit

SUBJECT F2 : ADVANCED FINANCIAL REPORTING

2.6 Bellamy Ltd is a large supermarket, operating in the UK. They receive payments from suppliers in return for advantageous shelf positioning and offering the suppliers' goods under promotional prices. Most of these suppliers sign 12 months contracts where payment is made up front. Bellamy has a policy of recognising the revenue from the supplier payments up front. The Financial Controller for Bellamy thinks that the recognition policy of the payments does not comply with IFRS 15. The Financial Controller approached the Finance Director with his views but was told "This is how we have always recognised these payments. They don't form part of our main operating income from selling goods so it will not really matter. IFRS 15 is not relevant here."

Which of the following statements are correct regarding the above scenario? Pick all that apply.

A   No ethical issues exist as the Finance Director is correct. IFRS 15 is not relevant.

B   The Financial Controller has a responsibility to follow the orders of the Finance Director and therefore no further action should be taken by the Financial Controller.

C   Revenue should be recognised from the contract as the risks and rewards associated with the goods sold to the supplier are transferred.

D   Revenue should be recognised in accordance to the stage of completion of the contract and the services are provided to the supplier.

E   There is an ethical risk that the Finance Director is deliberately overstating revenue. The Financial controller should contact the CIMA ethics helpline.

2.7 The following information in relation to Jolly has been obtained:

	20X8
Revenue	$975,000
Dividends received	$90,000
Dividends paid	$37,500
Cost of sales	$555,000
Finance costs	$45,000
Interest received	$31,500
Operating expenses	$300,000

What is the operating margin of Jolly?

A   8.5%

B   12.3%

C   17.9%

D   19.7%

OBJECTIVE TEST QUESTIONS : SECTION 1

2.8 The investors of JS require a return of 8% on their investment. The profits earned by the entity for the year ended 31st December 20X7 were $1.8m. The dividends for 20X7 were recently paid to the owners of JS's 1m ordinary shares. The dividend payment totalled $600,000. The dividends paid as a % of profits were consistent with previous payments. The ex div market price was $5.50.

What will be the growth rate used to calculate the cost of equity for JS? Answers are given to 1 decimal place.

A   2.7%
B   5.3%
C   8.0%
D   16.9%

2.9 KR had originally acquired 75% of the 200,000 $1 issued ordinary shares of AP for $1,845,000 on 1 Nov 20X6, when the balance on AP's reserves was $2,070,000. No fair value adjustments were considered necessary to AP's net assets at the date of acquisition.

KR disposed of 30% of the $1 ordinary shares in AP on 1 July 20X9 for $1,600,000 when AP's reserves were $3,000,000.

The fair value of the shareholding retained at 1 July 20X9 was $1,450,000.

The group policy is to value the non-controlling interest using the proportionate method. Goodwill has been fully impaired at the date of disposal.

Calculate the gain that would be recorded in the consolidated statement of profit or loss of the KR group upon the disposal of the shares in AP on 1 July 20X9.

(Give the answer to the nearest $. Show a gain as a positive figure and a loss as a negative figure.)

2.10 NCI in the LA group at 1 January 20X8 was $525,000. The NCI share of total comprehensive income for the year ended 31 December 20X8 was $201,000. A 90% subsidiary was disposed of during the year for proceeds of $750,000. NCI for this subsidiary is valued at fair value and on the disposal date the carrying amount was $64,500. NCI on 31 December 20X8 is $603,000.

What is the cash flow related to NCI that should be shown in the consolidated statement of cash flows of the LA group for the year ended 31 December 20X8?

A   A cash inflow of $750,000 in investing activities
B   A cash inflow of $750,000 in investing activities
C   A cash outflow of $214,500 in financing activities
D   A cash inflow of $214,500 in financing activities
E   A cash outflow of $187,500 in investing activities
F   A cash inflow of $187,500 in investing activities
G   A cash outflow of $58,500 in financing activities
H   A cash inflow of $58,500 in financing activities

RANDOM QUESTION TEST 3

3.1 The following ratios have been calculated for two companies in the same industry, Company H and Company C.

	H	C
Current ratio	1.6	1.4
Quick ratio	1.2	1.1
Trade receivables days	52 days	69 days

Fill in the gaps within the following statement using the options provided below to most accurately describe the liquidity of companies H and C.

more	less
higher	lower
longer	shorter

H is _____ liquid than C due to _____ levels of current assets compared to current liabilities.

C's liquidity could be improved if C could make its receivable days _____.

3.2 NW has in issue 200,000 $100 par value convertible bonds. The bonds are redeemable at a premium of 10% or convertible into 12 shares in 3 years' time. The current share price is $8.50 and dividends are expected to grow at 4% per annum.

In order to calculate the cost of debt in relation to the bonds, an IRR calculation will be required.

What value should be included as the cash flow on redemption per bond within the internal rate of return calculation?

A $100.00
B $102.00
C $110.00
D $114.74

3.3 SJ acquired 80% of the equity share capital of DA on 1st January 20X6. SJ's presentational currency and functional currency is the $. DA presents its financial statements in the dinar.

At the date of the acquisition, the book value of DA's assets was considered to be the same as their FV.

The carrying amount of DA's net assets in its financial statements at 31st December 20X8 is 3,000,000 dinar and its comprehensive income is 812,500 dinar.

Relevant exchange rates are as follows:

1st January 20X6 $1 = 15 dinar
31st December 20X7 $1 = 25 dinar
31st December 20X8 $1 = 20 dinar
Average rate for the year ended 31 December 20X8 $1 = 22 dinar

What is the annual exchange difference arising on the translation of the net assets of DA for inclusion in the SJ group financial statements for the year ended 31st December 20X8? No goodwill exchange impacts are required. Answers are given to the nearest $.

A $6,932 loss
B $6,932 gain
C $25,568 loss
D $25,568 gain
E $32,762 loss
F $32,762 gain

3.4 RX Ltd has issued 6% loan notes with a nominal value of $45,000 at 1st January 20X8.

Issue costs associated with the issue totalled $750. The effective interest rate for the loan notes is 8.5%.

What is the finance charge in the profit or loss account for the year ended 31st December 20X8 (to the nearest $)?

A $2,673
B $2,700
C $3,761
D $3,825

3.5 Moose Ltd leases an asset under a lease on 1st January 20X6. The lease term is for 5 years. The asset has an estimated useful life of 6 years and a current fair value of $89,000. The present value of the minimum lease payments is $87,000. Lease payments of $20,000 are made in arrears. The rate implicit with the lease is 4.8%

In accordance with IFRS 16, what is the current liability to be shown on the statement of financial positon as at the year ended 31st December 20X6?

A $16,483
B $16,584
C $54,592
D $56,789
E $71,176
F $73,272

3.6 LI has an 80% subsidiary, VE. LI also has an associate, RP with a 25% holding. During the year ended 31st December 20X6 the companies paid dividends of the following:

LI $1,800,000
VE $720,000
RP $360,000

What is the TOTAL for dividends paid in the consolidated statement of changes in equity of the LI group at 31st December 20X6?

A $2,466,000

B $2,376,000

C $1,944,000

D $1,800,000

3.7 Which of the following would reasonably be expected to cause the inventory days of a company to decrease from one year to the next?

A   Increased inventory obsolescence

B   Changing a key supplier

C   Slowdown in trading

D   A strategic decision to reduce selling prices

3.8 Which two of the following would be regarded as a related party of JO?

A   HN, a major customer of JO

B   The chief executive officer of the JO board

C   SH, an entity with which JO shares control of a joint venture

D   AR, an entity in which the wife of the chief executive officer of the JO board has a controlling shareholding

E   TT, JO's main banker

3.9 An entity has the following sources of finance, together with their related costs:

	Nominal value	Market value	Cost
Equity	$5 million	$15 million	13.2%
Irredeemable debt	$5 million	$7.5 million	8.4%
Redeemable debt	$5 million	$10 million	9.6%

What is the entity's weighted average cost of capital? Give your answer to 1 decimal place.

A   10.4%

B   10.8%

C   11.0%

D   11.3%

3.10 CV acquired a 10% investment in LP on 1 January 20X1 for $750,000. On 1 January 20X3, CV acquired an additional 60% of the equity share capital of LP at a cost of $5,625,000. The fair value of the original 10% investment at 1 January 20X2 was $1,387,500.

The fair value of the net assets of LP on 1 January 20X3 was $3,750,000. It is group policy to value non-controlling interest (NCI) at fair value at the date of acquisition. The fair value of the NCI in LP on 1 January 20X3 was $1,800,000.

The goodwill arising on the acquisition of LP that would be reflected in the consolidated financial statements of the CV group at 1 January 20X3 is:

A $3,675,000
B $4,425,000
C $5,062,500
D $6,000,000

RANDOM QUESTION TEST 4

The following scenario relates to questions 4.1 to 4.3 (3 questions)

SH is a listed entity that operates in the technology sector, developing wristbands to monitor customer fitness levels and sporting performance. A competitor has developed a cheaper and less cumbersome product called Sporty Ring, to be worn around the customer's pinky finger. This has proven very popular and has seen SH's market share eroded in the last few months of the financial period just ended 20X4.

Extracts from SH's financial information for the year are as follows:

	20X4	20X3
Revenue	$424m	$386m
Gross profit margin	22.4%	25.0%
Operating profit margin	4.2%	3.6%
Current ratio	1.5	2.2
Quick ratio	0.8	1.5
Inventories holding period	50 days	80 days
Receivables collection period	32.5 days	30 days
Payables payment period	78 days	54.5 days
Cash and cash equivalents	–	$12m
Short-term borrowings	$24m	–

SUBJECT F2 : ADVANCED FINANCIAL REPORTING

4.1 Which one of the following statements is the most valid conclusion that can be drawn from the above information and ratios?

A   The most likely reason for the reduction in gross profit margin is a reduction in selling prices

B   The most likely reason for the reduction in gross profit margin is a reduction in sales

C   The most likely reason for the reduction in gross profit margin is an increase in cost prices

D   The most likely reason for the reduction in gross profit margin is an increase in finance costs caused by the utilisation of an overdraft during 20X4

4.2 Which one of the following statements is a valid conclusion that can be drawn from the above ratios?

A   The decrease in inventory holding period has resulted in an increase in payable days

B   The decrease in inventory holding period has resulted in a fall in quick ratio

C   The decrease in the inventory holding period has been caused by increased sales during the period

D   The decrease in inventory holding period has resulted in a fall in cost of sales

4.3 Which one of the following statements is a valid conclusion that can be drawn from the above ratios?

A   SH has increased its marketing expenditure during the year to combat the impact of the new product in the market

B   SH operates in a marketplace that has shown growth in the last 12 months

C   The increase in payables payment period has been caused by an increase in the credit terms of SH's main suppliers

D   SH is insolvent as SH is overdrawn and its bank is looking for repayment of the overdraft

4.4 TS have just paid a dividend of 50 cents. The expected dividend growth rate is 7% and the cost of equity (ke) is 14.9%. The cum-div share price of TS is (to the nearest cent):

A $3.36

B $6.77

C $7.27

D $8.77

OBJECTIVE TEST QUESTIONS : SECTION 1

4.5 At 1st January 20X6, GP owned 80% of the ordinary share capital of MD.

On 1st April 20X6, GP disposed of 20% of MD's ordinary share capital for £385,000. The net assets of MD had a fair value of $2.2m. Goodwill was calculated using the FV method and had a carrying amount of $220,000 at the date of the disposal.

Which of the following double entries is posted to record the disposal as at 1st April 20X6?

A	Dr	Cash	385,000
	Dr	Equity	99,000
	Cr	NCI	484,000
B	Dr	Cash	385,000
	Dr	Equity	583,000
	Cr	NCI	968,000
C	Dr	NCI	484,000
	Cr	Equity	99,000
	Cr	Cash	385,000
D	Dr	NCI	968,000
	Cr	Equity	583,000
	Cr	Cash	385,000

4.6 CD invested $2.56 million in corporate bonds on 1 January 20X6. It paid commission of 0.5% on the transaction and it plans to retain the investment until the fixed redemption date of 31 December 20X9. This is in line with the strategy used for all of CD's debt financial assets.

The journal entry to record the transaction on 1 January 20X6 is:

A	Dr	Bank	$2,547,200
	Cr	Financial liability	$2,547,200
B	Dr	Bank	$2,572,800
	Cr	Financial liability	$2,572,800
C	Dr	Financial asset	$2,547,200
	Cr	Bank	$2,547,200
D	Dr	Financial asset	$2,572,800
	Cr	Bank	$2,572,800
E	Dr	P/l	$12,800
	Dr	Financial asset	$2,560,000
	Cr	Cash	$2,572,800

4.7 JS granted 2,000 share appreciation rights to each of its 360 employees on 1 January 20X1. If the share price exceeds $10 at the vesting date on 31 December 20X3, each employee would receive the excess as a cash payment for each of the rights they owned, as long as they are still employed on that date.

During X1, 20 people had left the company. As at 31 December X1, a further 40 were expected to leave by the vesting date.

During X2, 20 more had left and, as at the year-end X2, it was expected 10 more would leave during X3.

On 31 December 20X1, the FV of each SAR was $6; 31 December 20X2 the FV was $8 and on 31 December 20X3 the FV was $10.

What is the expense taken to profit and loss in the year ending 31/12/20X2? Give your answer to the nearest $.

4.8 On 30 June 20X4 HI acquired 800,000 of KL's 1 million shares. The purchase consideration was as follows:

HI issued 3 shares for every four shares acquired in KL. On 30 June the market price of a HI share was $3.80 and the market price of a KL share was $3.00.

HI agreed to pay $550,000 in cash to the existing shareholders on 30 June 20X5. HI's borrowing rate was 10% per annum.

HI paid advisors $100,000 for advice on the acquisition.

What is the cost of investment that will be used in the goodwill calculation in the consolidated accounts of HI?

    A $2,400,000
    B $2,780,000
    C $2,830,000
    D $2,880,000

4.9 Select which of the following statements are correct for a company listed on a stock exchange (select all that apply):

    A   A stock exchange listing enables an exact valuation of the company on any given day.
    B   Capital is more easily accessible for a company listed on a stock exchange.
    C   The process of gaining a listing is straightforward and inexpensive.
    D   More reporting is necessary for a public listed company.
    E   The original owners retain their control in the company when it floats on a stock exchange.

OBJECTIVE TEST QUESTIONS : SECTION 1

4.10 Which one of the following statements regarding the consolidated cash flow statement is true?

- A Impairment of goodwill is not a cash inflow or outflow and, as such, does not affect the consolidated cash flow statement
- B The gross amount of cash paid to acquire a subsidiary during the year is always shown under "cash flows from investing activities"
- C The dividend received from associates will be adjusted as part of the reconciliation to calculate "cash generated from operations"
- D Dividends paid to non-controlling interests will be presented under "cash flows from financing activities" on the face of the consolidated cash flow statement

RANDOM QUESTION TEST 5

The following scenario relates to questions 5.1 to 5.4 (4 questions)

DA acquired 75% of the $1m ordinary share capital of VI for $5m on 31st January 20X8. The retained earnings of VI at this date were $3,650,000.

VI owned 60% of the $2m ordinary share capital of BO. This investment occurred on the 31st January 20X6 when the retained earnings of BO were $2,500,000. The retained earnings of BO on 31st January 20X8 were $4,200,000. VI paid $8m for the shares of BO. The carrying amount of the assets of BO were equal to fair value at the date of acquisition apart from an item of non-depreciable land that had a fair value $450,000 in excess of its carrying amount.

DA group values goodwill using the proportionate method for VI and the fair value method for BO. The fair value of the non-controlling interests on the 31st January 20X8 for BO was $1,650,000: fair value of NCI for BO at 31st January 20X6 was $1,450,000. No impairment of goodwill was deemed necessary.

The DA group prepares their accounts to a year-end of 31st January. The current year end is 20X9. Retained earnings for DA, VI and BO as at 31st January 20X9 are $10,800,000, $5,250,000 and $3,250,000 respectively.

5.1 The indirect holding adjustment required in the calculation of the cost of investment for goodwill of BO will be:

- A $2,000,000
- B $2,800,000
- C $3,600,000
- D $4,400,000

SUBJECT F2 : ADVANCED FINANCIAL REPORTING

5.2 Which two of the following statements are true in relation to the DA group?

A   VI and BO will both be consolidated from the 31st January 20X8

B   The non-controlling interest of BO will use an effective shareholding of 45%

C   DA has control over VI and will consolidate VI as a subsidiary

D   DA exerts significant influence on BO and will apply equity accounting for BO

E   Any future impairment of the goodwill arising from both of the investments in VI and BO would require the impairment charges to be allocated between DA and the non-controlling interest of VI and BO

5.3 What would be the value of goodwill for BO as at 31st January 20X9?

A $300,000

B $1,000,000

C $2,700,000

D $4,700,000

5.4 What is the value of post-acquisition profits held in the DA group retained earnings as at 31st January 20X9 in relation to VI?

A $400,000

B $765,000

C $935,000

D $1,200,000

5.5 PH entered into a lease for a machine with a 3 year economic lifetime on 1 July 20X7 with the following terms:

- Three years non-cancellable lease
- Costs of arranging the lease are $2,000
- An initial deposit of $5,000
- Rent of $12,000 per annum payable
- Rate implicit with the lease of 10%

What is the carrying amount of the right-of-use asset as at the year ended 31 December 20X7?

A $19,896

B $24,563

C $29,844

D $30,703

OBJECTIVE TEST QUESTIONS : **SECTION 1**

5.6 **Which of the following is not a limitation of applying ratio analysis to published financial statements?**

- A Accounting policy choices can limit comparability between different companies
- B Financial statements may contain errors
- C Information within published financial statements is historic and out of date
- D Different ways of calculating certain ratios exist

5.7 Monkfish plc had profits after tax of $4.2 million in the year ended 31 December 20X7. On 1 January 20X7, Monkfish had 3.36 million ordinary shares in issue. On 1 April 20X7 Monkfish made a one for two rights issue at a price of $1.40 when the market price of Monkfish's shares was $2.00.

What is the basic earnings per share figure for the year ended 31 December 20X7, according to IAS 33 *Earnings per Share*?

- A 49.5 cents
- B 89.1 cents
- C 91.2 cents
- D 92.6 cents

5.8 BB has some 5% $100 loan notes in issue, which are redeemable in 3 years' time at a premium of 12.5%. The current market value of the loan notes is $98.

Using discount rates of 5% and 10%, calculate the yield to maturity (YTM) to two decimal places.

5.9 SE granted share options to all of its 400 employees on 1 January 20X1. Each employee will receive 500 share options provided they continue to be employed by SE for three years from the grant date. The fair value of an option was $1.60 at the grant date.

At 1 January 20X1 it was estimated that 90 staff would leave over the next three years.

24 staff left in the first year of the scheme and at 31 December 20X1 the revised estimate of staff expected to leave over the next two years was 56.

26 staff left in 20X2 and at 31 December 20X2, the revised estimate of staff expected to leave in the last year was 24.

The expense that would be recognised in relation to the option scheme in the year ended 31 December 20X2 is:

- A $173,867
- B $106,667
- C $88,534
- D $86,933
- E $85,333

SUBJECT F2 : ADVANCED FINANCIAL REPORTING

5.10 Which TWO of the following would not require disclosure within the consolidated financial statements of a group under IFRS® 12 *Disclosure of Interests in Other Entities*?

A   A investment in a subsidiary

B   A defined benefit pension plan

C   An investment in ordinary shares classified as FVOCI

D   An investment in an associate

E   An investment in an unconsolidated structured entity

Section 2

ANSWERS TO OBJECTIVE TEST QUESTIONS

SOURCES OF FINANCE

LONG TERM FINANCE

1 A, C

    B – Debt instruments can also be traded in the capital markets.

    D – An unlisted entity can issue shares, but not on the stock market.

    E – The primary function is to enable entities to raise finance, enabling investors to buy and sell investments is the secondary function.

2 General assets, less preferable

A floating charge is when debt is secured against **general assets** of the entity and this type of charge is considered **less preferable** from the lenders point of view to a fixed charge.

3 A

    B – Raising finance via a rights issue does not cause the flotation of an entity. Non-listed entities can issue rights issues to their current private shareholders. Flotation (being a publically listed entity) is not required to raise finance via a rights issue.

    C – Rights issues are made in proportion to shareholders' existing holdings therefore not resulting in a dilution to the percentage ownership.

    D – A rights issue is offered to all shareholders.

4 D

Theoretical ex rights price = $\dfrac{(5 \times \$2.75) + \$2.25}{6} = \$2.67$

5 Cum rights, ex rights

When a rights issue is announced, the existing shares will be traded **cum rights** up to the date of the issue. After the issue takes place, the shares will then be traded **ex rights**.

6 D

The directors are required to pay the preference dividend if they have sufficient distributable profits.

SUBJECT F2: ADVANCED FINANCIAL REPORTING

7   **C, D**

     C – Preference shareholders would be paid dividends in preference to ordinary shareholders.

     D – Ordinary dividends are not a fixed amount, they are determined by the directors.

8   **$7.31**

Theoretical ex rights price = $\dfrac{(3 \times \$7.50) + \$6.75}{4} = \$7.31$

9   **D**

The liability component of convertible debt must be recognised in the statement of financial position.

10   **More, uncertainty, equity, debt**

The providers of equity finance face **more** risk than the providers of debt finance because there is greater **uncertainty** over the level of their return. As a result **equity** providers will require a higher level of return on their investment than **debt** providers.

COST OF CAPITAL AND YIELD TO MATURITY

11   **8.7%**

$k_e = \dfrac{0.60}{(7.50 - 0.60)} = 8.7\%$

12   **D**

$k_e = \dfrac{0.10 \times 1.03}{\text{ex-div price}} + 0.03 = 0.15$

Therefore, ex-div price = $\dfrac{0.10 \times 1.03}{0.15 - 0.03} = 0.86$

13   **Ex div market price**

When calculating the cost of preference shares, the dividend is divided by the **ex div market price** of the preference share.

14   **6.3%**

Yield to maturity = $6/94.5 \times 100 = 6.3\%$

15   **8.9%**

$k_e = \dfrac{0.10 \times 1.03}{1.86 - 0.10} + 0.03 = 8.9\%$

16   **$109.50**

Cash option = $\$100 \times 102\% = \$102$

Shares option = $15 \times (\$6 \times 1.04^5) = \$109.50$

Assume that investor will choose higher value option.

ANSWERS TO OBJECTIVE TEST QUESTIONS : SECTION 2

17 B

Post-tax cost of debt = (5 × 80%)/88 = 4.5%

18 B

The relevant cash outflows would be the annual interest payment **net of tax**, not gross, and the redemption value.

19 7.5%

Yield to maturity = 7/92.75 × 100 = 7.5%

20 A

$$k_e = \frac{divi \times 1.04}{6.50} + 0.04 = 0.125$$

Therefore, $divi = \frac{(0.125 - 0.04) \times 6.50}{1.04} = 0.53$

21 $2.73

$$k_e = \frac{0.13 \times 1.05}{\text{current price}} + 0.05 = 0.10$$

Therefore, current price = $\frac{0.13 \times 1.05}{0.10 - 0.05} = 2.73$

22 4.1%

Post-tax cost of debt = (6 × 70%)/102 = 4.1%

23 D

Cash option = $100 × 115% = $115

Shares option = 10 × ($10.22 × 1.02^5) = $112.84

Assume that investor will choose higher value option.

24 13.2%

WACC = (15% × 4/5) + (8% × 75% × 1/5) = 12% + 1.2% = 13.2%

25 D

Source	Market value $m	Proportion	Cost of capital %	Weighted cost %
Ordinary shares (10 × 1.20)	12	0.632	11.7	7.4
Long dated bonds (8 × 0.875)	7	0.368	6	2.2
	19	1		9.6

26 D

$K_d = (7 \times 70\%)/96 = 5.1\%$

$K_e = 0.50 / (3.80 - 0.50) = 15.2\%$

27 6%

Post-tax cost of debt = (coupon rate × 75%)/92 = 4.89%

Therefore, coupon rate = 0.0489 × 92/0.75 = 6%

28 C

$$k_e = \frac{0.12 \times 1.05}{1.22} + 0.05 = 15.3\%$$

Dividend per share in above calculation = 120,000/1m = 0.12

29 C

A, B and D are all considered to be benefits/uses of WACC.

C is a limitation as the WACC should ideally reflect market values.

30 8.7%

Yield to maturity (IRR) = $5\% + \frac{12.91}{(12.91 + 4.65)} \times (10\% - 5\%) = 8.7\%$

FINANCIAL REPORTING (I)

INTERNATIONAL ACCOUNTING STANDARDS

IAS 32 & 39 *FINANCIAL INSTRUMENTS*

31 Asset, equity, obligation, unfavourable

'A financial instrument is any contract that gives rise to a financial <u>asset</u> of one entity and a financial liability or <u>equity</u> instrument of another entity.

A financial liability is any liability that is a contractual <u>obligation</u> to deliver cash or another financial asset to another entity or to exchange financial assets or liabilities under <u>unfavourable</u> conditions'(IAS 32, para 11).

32 B

Finance costs recognised by ROB are:

	$
Issue costs	100,000
Interest paid (4m × 5%)	200,000
	300,000

The finance costs that should have been recognised are:

	$
(4m – 100,000) × 8.5%	331,500

Therefore, the correct journal entry to correct the accounting treatment is:

			$
Dr	Finance costs		31,500
Cr	Liability		31,500

33 $9,342,264

Initial recognition of liability will be total cash received less equity component.
Liability should then be subsequently measured at amortised cost.

	$
Opening liability (10m – 794,200)	9,205,800
Finance cost at effective rate (9,205,800 × 8%)	736,464
Cash paid (10m × 6%)	(600,000)
Liability at 31 December 20X3	9,342,264

34 $5,840

	$
Initial measurement at acquisition (40,000 × $2.68 × 1.05)	112,560
Fair value at 31 July 20X2 (40,000 × $2.96)	118,400
Gain	5,840

Transaction costs are added to FVOCI assets upon initial recognition.

35 The liability for this instrument at 31 December 20X1 will be calculated as follows:

Liability		$
Opening balance	(3.4m – 200,000)	**3,200,000**
Plus: finance cost	(3.2m × 7.05%)	**225,600**
Less: interest paid	(3.4m × 6%)	**(204,000)**
Closing balance		X

36 B

A is not appropriate as the loans to employees are not held for trading purposes.

C is not appropriate as the loans to employees are not held with the intention to hold some and sell some of the loans.

D is not appropriate as the loans are financial assets, not financial liabilities.

37 D

Cumulative preference shares should be recognised as a financial liability as there is an obligation to pay the dividends (due to them being cumulative). Therefore A is incorrect and D would be correct. The dividend paid would be recorded as finance costs to match the treatment of the instrument as a liability.

Cumulative preference shares allow dividends to deferred and paid cumulatively in periods of poor liquidity. Non-cumulative irredeemable preference shares would lose their right to dividend if AB decided to forego a dividend payment. Cumulative preference shares are less risky than non-cumulative preference shares. Therefore B is incorrect.

AB has issued the preference shares in order to raise finance, rather than acquiring them as an investment. Therefore C is incorrect.

38 $23,000

As the FVOCI financial asset is an investment in debt, upon disposal of the investment, the gains or losses held within reserves will be recycled to profit or loss.

	$
Sale proceeds	65,000
Less carrying amount of investment at disposal (42,000 + 18,000)	(60,000)
Add gain reclassified from other components of equity	18,000
Total gain in profit or loss at disposal	23,000

Tutorial note: If the FVOCI investment was in shares (equity), the gains or losses held in reserves would not be reclassified to profit or loss on disposal. They would be reclassified into retained earnings.

39

The journal entry required to record the subsequent measurement of the shares at 31 December 20X1 is:

	Account reference	$
Debit	Investment in shares	310,000
Credit	**Profit or loss**	

Transaction costs are expensed upon initial recognition of a held for trading (fair value through profit or loss) financial asset.

40 A

	$
Contracted purchase price (1,000 × $1,200)	1,200,000
Equivalent purchase price at reporting date (1,000 × $1,280)	1,280,000
Gain on contract (therefore favourable terms)	80,000

ANSWERS TO OBJECTIVE TEST QUESTIONS : SECTION 2

41 C

As the factor can recover the cash advance if the customer fails to settle the receivable balance after 6 months, RF is still exposed to the significant risks of ownership and therefore should not derecognise the receivable balance upon receipt of the advance. Instead, the cash inflow should be recognised as a liability (secured on the receivable balance). Dr Cash $7,650,000 Cr Liability $7,650,000.The receivable is not derecognised and no expense is initially recorded. As such C is incorrect. The admin fee is a finance cost and is recorded using the effective interest rate over the life of the arrangement.

42 B

The preference shares are redeemable and should therefore be classified as a financial liability.

Issue costs are deducted from the initial recognition of the redeemable preference shares:

	$
Cash received	5,000,000
Less issue costs incurred	(200,000)
Initial measurement of preference shares	4,800,000

The correct journal entry to correct the accounting treatment is therefore:

		$
Dr	Bank	4,800,000
Cr	Financial liability	4,800,000

43 C

The investment is a financial asset which would be measured at amortised cost. MAT's intention is to hold until the maturity date, passing the business model test. All cash flows are capital and interest, passing the contractual cash flow tests. Any transaction costs should be added to the asset on initial recognition.

	$
Amount paid for investment	2,000,000
Transaction costs incurred	100,000
Initial measurement of financial asset	2,100,000

The correct journal entry to correct the accounting treatment is:

		$
Dr	Investment	2,100,000
Cr	Bank	2,100,000

SUBJECT F2 : ADVANCED FINANCIAL REPORTING

44 **B**

	$
PV of principal after 4 years = $6m × 0.708	4,248,000
PV of interest of 7% on $6m for 4 years = $6m × 7% × 3.24	1,360,800
Initial measurement of liability component	5,608,800

Equity = $6m – $5,608,800 = $391,200

45 **D**

	A$
Contracted purchase price (2m/0.64)	3,125,000
Equivalent purchase price at reporting date (2m/0.70)	2,857,143
Loss on contract (therefore unfavourable terms)	267,857

46 The impact of the investment in the statement of profit or loss for the year ended 30 June 20X1 is:

Statement of profit or loss extract	$
Profit from operations	X
Finance income (4.2m × 8.4%)	**352,800**
Finance costs	**BLANK**
	—
Profit before tax	X
Other comprehensive income	
Gain on revaluation of FVOCI financial asset	**227,200**

The debt instrument is classified as fair value through other comprehensive income (FVOCI) as the business intends to both sell and hold its debt financial assets.

Initial recognition of the financial asset will be at fair value (typically cost) plus any transaction costs. For the FVOCI asset = $4,000,000 + $200,000 = $4,200,000,

The subsequent treatment of the FVOCI financial asset is to revalue to fair value, gains or losses to other comprehensive income.

As this is a debt instrument, finance income and coupon rate receipts will still need to be recorded.

The effective rate applied to the opening measurement is finance income as the investment is a financial asset (not a financial liability).

ANSWERS TO OBJECTIVE TEST QUESTIONS : SECTION 2

To work out entries to record the FVOCI debt financial asset, the following working will be required:

B/f	Interest at effective rate (8.4%)	Receipt at coupon (7%)	Sub-total	Gain held in OCI (β)	Fair value
4,200,000	352,800	(280,000)	4,272,800	227,200	4,500,000

47 The journal entry required to record the subsequent measurement of the investment at 30 June 20X2 is:

	Account reference	$
Debit	Investment in shares	**122,000**
Credit	**Reserves**	

The investment is classified as FVOCI. As a result, transaction costs are added to the asset at initial recognition. Subsequent measurement is at fair value with changes in value being recorded in reserves.

	$
Initial recognition of investment (2,400,000 × 1.02)	2,448,000
Fair value at reporting date	2,570,000
Gain on re-measurement	122,000

48 The journal entry required to initially record the convertible bond on 1 January 20x2 is:

	Account reference	$
Debit	**Bank**	4,000,000
Credit	**Financial liability**	**3,689,200**
Credit	Equity	**310,800**

Tutorial note:

The calculation of the liability and equity component is provided below however you would not need to perform this calculation to answer the question. A convertible bond is part liability and part equity and the liability component will always be the higher of the two values – if you know this then there is only one valid option which is to include 3,689,200 as the liability component and 310,800 as the equity component.

Calculation (as proof of figures)

	$
PV of principal after 5 years = $4m × 0.65	2,600,000
PV of interest of 7% on $4m for 5 years = $4m × 7% × 3.89	1,089,200
Initial measurement of liability component	3,689,200

Equity component = $4m − $3,689,200 = $310,800

SUBJECT F2 : ADVANCED FINANCIAL REPORTING

IFRS 2 SHARE-BASED PAYMENTS

49 $141,050

	$
Cumulative expense at 31 July 20X2:	
(500 – 20 – 18 – 30) × 1,000 × FV$1.30 × 2/4	280,800
Less expense recognised in y/e 31 July 20X1:	
(500 – 20 – 50) × 1,000 × FV$1.30 × ¼	(139,750)
Expense in y/e 31 July 20X2	141,050

50 **Equity-settled, equity, grant date, cash-settled, liabilities, reporting date**

In accordance with IFRS 2 *Share-based payments*:

A share option scheme is an example of a/an **equity-settled** share-based payment, in which an expense should be recognised with an associated credit to **equity** measured using the fair value at the **grant date**.

A share appreciation rights scheme is an example of a/an **cash-settled** share-based payment, in which an expense should be recognised with an associated credit to **liabilities** measured using the fair value at the **reporting date**.

51 D

	$
Liability at 30 June 20X2:	
(500 – 42 – 28 – 25) × 1,000 × FV$11 × 2/3	2,970,000

52 B

	$
Expense for y/e 31 December 20X0:	
(400 – 22 – 56) × 1,000 × FV$2.20 × 1/4	177,100

53 The journal entry required to record the charge to kl's profit or loss for the year ended 30 November 20x9 in respect of the SARs will be:

	Account reference	$
Debit	Profit or loss	**555,000**
Credit	**Non-current liabilities**	

	$
Cumulative expense at 30 November 20X9:	
(120 – 12 – 8 – 10) × 1,000 × FV$17 × 2/3	1,020,000
Less expense recognised in y/e 30 November 20X8:	
(120 – 12 – 15) × 1,000 × FV$15 × 1/3	(465,000)
Expense in y/e 30 November 20X9	555,000

IAS 33 *EARNINGS PER SHARE*

54   50.7 cents

Basic EPS = $3.8m/(5m × 3/2) = 50.7 cents

55   B

Earnings = $6,582,000 – $420,000 = $6,162,000

Weighted average number of shares:

Brought forward	8,000,000
Market price issue (5/12 × 2,400,000)	1,000,000
	9,000,000

Basic EPS = $6,162,000/9,000,000 = 68.5 cents

56   3,694,349

Weighted average number of shares:

Prior to rights issue	3m × 1/12 × 7.5/7.3	256,849
After rights issue	3m × 5/4 × 11/12	3,437,500
		3,694,349

57   D

Dilutive shares:	
Share held under option	1,000,000
Shares that would have been issued at market price (1m × 3.1/4)	(775,000)
Shares effectively issued for no consideration	225,000

Diluted EPS = $3.5m/(7m + 225,000) = 48.4 cents

SUBJECT F2 : ADVANCED FINANCIAL REPORTING

58 **$862,500**

Weighted average number of shares:		
Brought forward	10,000,000	
Market price issue (9/12 × 2,000,000)	1,500,000	
		11,500,000
Bonus issue		× 5/4
		14,375,000

Basic EPS = 6 cents = profit/14,375,000
Therefore profit = 14,375,000 × $0.06 = $862,500

59 **28.8 cents**

	$
Adjusted earnings:	
Per basic eps	3,000,000
Interest on convertible instrument ($5m × 6% × 75%)	225,000
	3,225,000

Diluted EPS = $3,225,000/(10m + 1.2m) = 28.8 cents

60 **A, D**

Irredeemable preference dividends relating to previous years will have been deducted from previous years' earnings. Therefore B is incorrect.

Ordinary dividends are distributions of earnings, not part of the calculation. Therefore C is incorrect.

Redeemable preference dividends will be recognised as a finance cost within profit or loss and therefore will already be reflected in the profit after tax figure.

61 **B**

Comparative EPS = last years' EPS × rights bonus fraction inverted
Rights bonus fraction = CRP/TERP = 2.2/2.06
Therefore, comparative EPS = 46.2 cents × 2.06/2.2 = 43.3 cents

62 **78.6 cents**

Comparative EPS = last years' EPS × bonus fraction inverted
There is no restatement with respect to a full market price issue
Therefore, comparative EPS = 98.2 cents × 4/5 = 78.6 cents

ANSWERS TO OBJECTIVE TEST QUESTIONS : SECTION 2

63 B

Dilutive shares:

Share held under option	1,500,000
Shares that would have been issued at market price (1.5m × 3.5/4.75)	(1,105,263)
Shares effectively issued for no consideration	394,737

IFRS 16 *LEASES*

64 $15,949

Lease liability = present value of lease rentals for 4 years discounted using rate implicit with the lease of 9%.
$70,000 × 3.240 = $226,800

Subsequent treatment – add finance cost less rental repayments

Year	Bal b/f $	Interest at 9% $	Paid $	Bal c/f $
20X1	226,800	20,412	(70,000)	177,212
20X2	177,212	**15,949**	(70,000)	123,161

65 A, C, E

In accordance with IFRS 16 *Leases*, lessors must consider whether a lease is a finance lease or an operating lease. A finance lease is one in which the significant risks and rewards of ownership of the leased asset have transferred to the lessee.

If the lessor (FL) is responsible for maintenance and repair this would suggest that the risk of damage and breakdown has not been transferred to the lessee (JS). Therefore B is incorrect.

The sale at the end of the lease is at normal commercial terms. Being able to buy the asset at market value does not suggest either a risk or reward of ownership. There is no benefit or downside from the condition. Therefore D is not an indicator of risk or reward transfer and, consequently, of the presence of a finance lease.

66

The table below provides a summary of accounting treatments prescribed by IFRS 16 *Leases* of sale and leaseback arrangements.

Sale and leaseback where the sale price of the asset is equal to fair value.	D
Sale and leaseback where the sale price of the assets is above fair value.	A
Sale and leaseback where the sale price is lower than the carrying amount.	C
Sale and leaseback where the sale does not meet the requirements of a sale as per IFRS 15 *Revenue from contracts with customers*.	B

SUBJECT F2 : ADVANCED FINANCIAL REPORTING

67 **$56,250**

	$
Total lease payments (9 × $125,000)	1,125,000
Lease term	/10 years
Annual charge to profit or loss	112,500

Charge in year ended 31 December 20X1 = 6/12 × 112,500 = $56,250

68 **A**

Initial value of liability = present value of lease rentals for 5 years discounted using rate implicit with the lease 7%

$110,000 × 4.100 = $451,000

Year	Bal b/f	Interest at 7%	Paid	Bal c/f
	$	$	$	$
20X1	451,000	31,570	(110,000)	372,570
20X2	372,570	26,080	(110,000)	**288,650**

Non-current liability = amount outstanding after next year's payment

Direct costs would be capitalised as part of the right-of-use asset, not the lease liability.

IFRS 15 REVENUE FROM CONTRACTS WITH CUSTOMERS

69 **A, E**

For revenue to be recorded, a contract must exist and the distinct performance obligations of the contract must be identified.

Performance obligations do not always need to be fully satisfied for revenue to be recorded. If performance obligations are satisfied over time, revenue from the contract can be allocated across a period of time. Option B is incorrect.

Variable consideration can be included within revenue if it is highly probable to not reverse. It is not a requirement for revenue to be recorded. Every contract does not need an element of variable consideration. Option C is incorrect.

It is the transfer of control, rather than the delivery itself, that are conditions that must be satisfied in accordance with IFRS 15. It is possible for no control transfer to have occurred despite the goods already being delivered e.g. sale or return arrangements. D is not always correct.

70 **D**

The directors are required to act in the best interests of the shareholders, not themselves. They are not complying with international accounting standards, which would require the sale and repurchase agreement to be recognised as a loan and the fact that they have previously used the correct accounting treatment demonstrates that they are knowingly overstating profits, rather than it being from a lack of knowledge. This would be considered unethical.

ANSWERS TO OBJECTIVE TEST QUESTIONS : SECTION 2

71   B

Revenue can be recorded over time if the customer simultaneously receives and consumes the benefits provided by the seller. The support service would meet this condition and be recorded over the 3 years that the support is provided.

Revenue is recorded at a point in time if control of the good is transferred to the customer. As a result of the software being developed and delivered on 30th June 20X3, then revenue is recorded in full at that date.

	$
Revenue from sale of goods (software)	500,000
Revenue from provision of service (75,000/3 years × 6/12)	12,500
Total revenue to be recognised in year ended 31 December 20X3	512,500

72   B

The right of return indicates that SB have retained the risk of obsolescence.

A is incorrect as this would suggest that JK are exposed to the risk or benefits from changes in selling price.

C is incorrect as this would suggest that JK are exposed to the risk of theft and damage.

D is incorrect as this would suggest that JK have benefits of ownership.

73   A

There is a requirement to repurchase the land and therefore DRT should not derecognise it. If the option to repurchase is not exercised over the next four years then DRT will have an obligation to repurchase it at the end of the four year period. Therefore, control is not passed to NKL and revenue is not recorded. Further indications that control has not been transferred include the requirement for NKL to seek DRT approval before using the land. DRT should continue to recognise the land as an asset and should record a liability for the repurchase.

74   C

The sale of goods XZ from to WY would record revenue at a point in time. The revenue should only be recognised when control of the goods have transferred to WY. Control of the goods does not transfer to WY until either the end of the 28 day period or the onward sale to a customer of WY. Therefore, the revenue for the sale of the remaining 38% of the goods cannot be recognised even if it is considered likely that one of these two events will occur.

However, XZ would be able to recognise revenue for the goods that WY has sold on and therefore C is true.

Revenue = 62% × $1,250,000 = $775,000

XZ should continue to recognise the goods not sold on in its inventory until the risks and rewards transfer.

The cost of these goods = $1,250,000 × 75% × 38% = $356,250, therefore D is not true.

75 $1.9M

In 20X1:

Total expected profit = 40m − 7m − 26m = $7 million

Stage of completion = 8/40 = 20%

Profit recognised = 20% × $7m = $1.4 million

In 20X2:

Total expected profit = 40m − 18m − 16m = $6 million

Stage of completion = 22/40 = 55%

Cumulative profit to be recognised = 55% × $6m = $3.3 million

Therefore, profit to be recognised in 20X2 = $3.3m − $1.4m = $1.9 million

76 C

	$000
Costs incurred to date	5,100
Profit recognised to date	1,700
Less progress billings to date	(6,000)
Contract asset	800

77 B

	$000	$000
Contract price		3,000
Costs:		
Incurred to date – re work completed	1,500	
Inventory not yet used	150	
To complete	350	
		(2,000)
Total expected profit		1,000

Percentage complete = 1,500/2,000 = 75%

Therefore profit = 75% × $1,000,000 = $750,000

78 A, C, E

	$m
Contract price	26
Costs incurred to date	(17)
Costs to complete	(11)
Expected loss	(2)

Loss making contract therefore statement of profit or loss extract:

	$m
Revenue (= work certified)	14
Cost of sales (balancing figure)	(16)
Loss	(2)

and statement of financial position extract is:

	$m
Costs to date	17
Loss	(2)
Progress billings	(12)
Asset/amounts due from customer	3

IAS 37 PROVISIONS, CONTINGENT LIABILITIES AND CONTINGENT ASSETS

79 C

Future operating losses are specifically prohibited by IAS 37 *Provisions, contingent liabilities and contingent assets*. No provision should be made as there is no obligation.

80 D

If ES have created a valid expectation that they will incur costs to clean-up such leaks in their environmental and social report, they will have created a constructive obligation and therefore should make a provision. The leak has already occurred and therefore there is a past event giving rise to the obligation.

A is incorrect as there does not have to be a legal obligation; it could be a constructive obligation instead as discussed above.

B is incorrect as an estimate has been made of the costs and therefore, provided there is an obligation, a provision would be required rather than a contingent liability.

C is incorrect as an intention is not sufficient to make a provision; there must be an obligation.

81 The IAS 37 *Provisions, contingent liabilities and contingent assets* accounting treatment can be summarised as follows:

Degree of probability of an outflow/inflow of resources	Liability	Asset
Virtually certain	Recognise	Recognise
Probable	Make provision	Disclose (in note)
Possible	Disclose (in note)	Ignore
Remote	Ignore	Ignore

IAS 12 *TAXATION*

82 **A, C**

In the other three situations, the carrying amount of the asset is greater than its tax base and therefore a deferred tax liability exists.

83 **B**

Deferred tax liability at 31 December 20X3 = (470,000 – 365,000) × 20% = $21,000

Therefore, reduction in deferred tax liability in year = $4,000 => credit in profit or loss

84 **B, C, D**

The additional temporary difference created by the revaluation is $350,000. The additional deferred tax liability arising on this is $70,000. Therefore A is incorrect.

	Before revaluation $000	After revaluation $000
Carrying amount of PPE	400	750
Tax base	(370)	(370)
Temporary difference	30	380
Deferred tax liability at 20%	6	76

The increase in liability from $4,000 (b/f) to $6,000 (above) is charged to profit or loss.

The additional $70,000 created by the revaluation is charged to other comprehensive income and debited to the revaluation reserve.

Therefore, the balance on the revaluation reserve = 350,000 – 70,000 = $280,000

85 **C**

There is a deductible temporary difference resulting in a deferred tax asset. The temporary difference is based on the intrinsic value of the share options, rather than the fair value at grant which is the basis for the profit or loss charge.

ANSWERS TO OBJECTIVE TEST QUESTIONS : SECTION 2

86 Taxable, liability

If the carrying amount of an asset exceeds its tax base then there is a **taxable** temporary difference and this will result in a deferred tax **liability**.

IAS 24 *RELATED PARTIES*

87 A, B, F

The above are specifically defined as related parties.

C and D are specifically excluded from the definition of a related party.

Employees would not be considered to be a related party unless they were members of key management personnel.

88 B

Subsidiaries, associates and joint ventures are all related parties.

Two venturers who have joint control of an entity are excluded from the definition, therefore AB and PQ would not be considered to be related parties.

FINANCIAL REPORTING (II)

CONSOLIDATED FINANCIAL STATEMENTS

BASIC GROUPS

89 C

Although the transaction would not affect the consolidated financial statements, it would affect the subsidiary's individual financial statements and is an attempt to mislead any potential acquirers.

The transaction would have to be disclosed as a related party transaction. For users to understand the impact of the transaction on profit they would need to be made aware of the inflated prices however LP are not planning to disclose any information about the price increase.

90 C

In accordance with IFRS 3 *Business* combinations, any contingent consideration should be recognised at fair value in the goodwill calculation.

Tutorial note:

The extent of probability would be reflected in the fair value of the contingent consideration.

SUBJECT F2 : ADVANCED FINANCIAL REPORTING

91 D

	$000
Book value	850
Fair value uplift to PPE	650
Fair value uplift to inventory	25
Contingent liability	(100)
Fair value of net assets at acquisition	1,425

92 A

Additional depreciation = 650,000/5 = $130,000

The contingent liability would be updated to its fair value of $110,000 in the consolidated statement of financial position. Therefore B is incorrect.

The change in the fair value of the contingent liability should be recognised in post-acquisition profit, not as an adjustment to goodwill at acquisition. Therefore C is incorrect.

The $25,000 additional value of inventory would create an additional cost of sale in the consolidated statement of profit or loss and therefore would result in an additional debit, rather than credit, upon sale of the inventory. Therefore D is incorrect.

93 $85,000

	$000	$000
Consideration paid		1,750
Fair value of NCI		320
Less fair value of net assets at acquisition:		
Share capital	1,000	
Retained earnings	920	
Fair value uplift (745 – 680)	65	
		(1,985)
Goodwill at acquisition and at reporting date		85

94 B

Non-controlling interest:	$
Fair value of NCI at acquisition	320,000
NCI share of post-acquisition reserves	
20% × 110,250 (see below)	22,050
	342,050

Post-acquisition reserves of FZ:	$
Retained earnings at reporting date	1,100,000
Less retained earnings at acquisition	(920,000)
Fair value depreciation: 65,000/5 × 9/12	(9,750)
Unrealised profit: 300,000 × 20%	(60,000)
	110,250

95 A, D, E

The group share of FZ's post-acquisition earnings will be credited, not debited, to consolidated retained earnings. Therefore B is incorrect.

The impact that the unrealised profit adjustment has on consolidated retained earnings is $48,000 (80% × $60,000). As the subsidiary made the profit, 20% of the unrealised amount will be deducted from non-controlling interests, with the parent's share being deducted from consolidated retained earnings. Therefore C is incorrect.

Tutorial note:

The same applies to the fair value depreciation, with 80% of the amount being charged to consolidated retained earnings. Therefore both D and E are correct.

96 $4,375,000

Property, plant and equipment at 31 December 20X2:	$000
JK	3,300
LM	850
Fair value uplift (1,100,000 FV – (500,000 + 350,000) book value)	250
Fair value depreciation (250,000 above × 1/10)	(25)
	4,375

Tutorial note:

The fair value uplift is calculated by deducting the book value of net assets from the fair value. The fair value is given in the question as $1,100,000 and the book value is the share capital of 500,000 plus the reserves at acquisition of $350,000.

97 B

Fair value of consideration paid:	$000
Shares 500,000 × $3.50	1,750
Cash	408
Deferred consideration 1,000,000 × 0.842 (9% discount for 2 years)	842
Legal and professional fees – don't include (should be expensed)	–
	3,000

98 $44,000

	$
Fair value of non-controlling interest at acquisition (20% × 500,000 × $1.80)	180,000
Value of non-controlling interest using proportion of net assets (20% × 680,000)	(136,000)
	44,000

Tutorial note:

The only difference in goodwill between the two methods is the value used for the non-controlling interest at acquisition. Therefore the above calculation is all that's needed to answer the question.

99 Arrangement, operation, venture

As per IFRS 11 *Joint arrangements*:

A joint arrangement is an arrangement of which two parties or more have joint control. A joint operation is where the parties that have joint control have rights to the assets, and obligations for the liabilities, relating to the arrangement. A joint venture is where the parties that have joint control have rights to the net assets of the arrangement.

ANSWERS TO OBJECTIVE TEST QUESTIONS : SECTION 2

100 B

	$000	$000
Consideration paid		3,250
Fair value of NCI		1,325
Less fair value of net assets at acquisition:		
Share capital	1,000	
Retained earnings	1,500	
Fair value uplift (1,600 – 1,200)	400	
		(2,900)
Goodwill at acquisition		1,675
Less impairment		(425)
Goodwill at the reporting date		1,250

101 C, E

The fair value adjustment relates to non-depreciable property and will not affect the post-acquisition reserves of HD or the consolidated retained earnings of the ZB group. Therefore C is incorrect.

As the non-controlling interest is measured at fair value at acquisition, only ZB's share of the impairment will be charged to consolidated retained earnings = 70% × $425,000 = $297,500. Therefore E is incorrect.

102 C

Non-controlling interest:	$
Fair value of NCI at acquisition	1,325,000
NCI share of post-acquisition reserves	
30% × (2,750,000 – 1,500,000)	375,000
NCI share of goodwill impairment	
30% × 425,000	(127,500)
	1,572,500

103 A

Post-acquisition reserves of FG:	$
Total comprehensive income for year (acquired one year ago)	125,000
Fair value depreciation	(30,000)
Goodwill impairment	(15,000)
	80,000
Group share	× 65%
	52,000

Tutorial note:

As the subsidiary was acquired exactly one year ago, the calculation above is similar to that we would perform to calculate the NCI share of total comprehensive income for the year. The only difference here is that we are calculating the group share rather than the NCI share.

If the subsidiary is acquired more than one year ago and we're calculating the amount that would appear in consolidated reserves we would need to include cumulative figures to date. We would start with reserves at the reporting date, deduct reserves at acquisition and then adjust for cumulative consolidation adjustments to date, i.e. depreciation, impairment etc.

104 C

The associate has made the sales to the parent, therefore the unrealised profit should be deducted from the associate's profit and the parent's (and therefore group) inventory.

The unrealised profit is calculated as follows:

	$
Sales value of goods still held: 200,000/2	100,000
Profit on above sales: 100,000 × 25%	25,000
Group share: 25,000 × 35%	8,750

105 A, D, F

Goodwill impairment only affects the non-controlling interest if the fair value method has been used to measure the non-controlling interest at acquisition. Therefore B is incorrect.

Provisions for unrealised profits only affect the non-controlling interest if the subsidiary made the profit on the transaction. If the parent made the sales the non-controlling interest is not affected, therefore C is incorrect.

The non-controlling interest's share of any dividend paid by the subsidiary would be reflected in the consolidated statement of changes in equity. It is the parent's share that would be eliminated upon consolidation. Therefore E is incorrect.

106 B

NCI share of total comprehensive income:	$
Subsidiary TCI (post-acquisition) = 90,000 × 9/12	67,500
Fair value depreciation	(20,000)
Goodwill impairment	(30,000)
	17,500
NCI share	× 20%
	3,500

ANSWERS TO OBJECTIVE TEST QUESTIONS : SECTION 2

Tutorial note:

The provision for unrealised profit is not included in the above calculation as the parent made the profit and therefore the adjustment does not affect the subsidiary's total comprehensive income.

107 B, C, D

Any profit on the sale of goods by the parent to the subsidiary would be deducted from the total comprehensive income attributable to the parent shareholders, not the NCI. Therefore A is incorrect.

The dividend paid by SU is reflected as a distribution of profit rather than part of profit in SU's financial statements. Therefore its elimination does not affect the NCI calculation and E is incorrect.

108 $720,000

	$000
Net assets of TR at reporting date:	
Book value	2,500
Fair value uplift	475
Fair value depreciation 475 × 4/20	(95)
	2,880
NCI share	× 25%
NCI at reporting date	720

Tutorial note:

As the NCI is measured using the proportion of net assets method, the NCI at the reporting date will be the NCI share of the net assets at the reporting date, as shown above. An alternative way to calculate this is below. Note that goodwill impairment is not included in the calculation as it is all charged to consolidated reserves when NCI is measured using the proportionate method.

	$000
NCI at acquisition 25% × (1,220 + 475 FV)	423.75
NCI share of post-acquisition reserves	
25% × (2,500 – 1,220)	320
NCI share of FV depreciation	
25% × (475 × 4/20)	(23.75)
NCI at reporting date	720

111

109 $8,180,000

Property, plant and equipment at 31 December 20X2:	$000
ER	5,900
MR	2,000
Fair value uplift	400
Fair value depreciation (400,000 × 3/10)	(120)
	8,180

110 C

NCI share of profit:	$
Subsidiary profit (post-acquisition) = 180,000 × 6/12	90,000
Fair value depreciation	(15,000)
Unrealised profit = 100,000 × 30% × 30%	(9,000)
	66,000
NCI share	× 25%
	16,500

Tutorial note:

The goodwill impairment is not included in the calculation as the non-controlling interest is measured using the proportionate method and therefore all impairment is allocated to the profit attributable to parent shareholders.

111 B

The dividend would not have been in WeeJoe's statement of profit or loss. Brendan's share would be removed from consolidated investment income as Brendan will have recorded the income in its individual financial statements. The associate's profits are not affected.

The PUP adjustment is calculated as follows:

	$	%
Sales	25,000	125
Cost of sales	(20,000)	100
Gross profit	5,000	25
80% left in Brendan's inventory	4,000	
Unrealised element (P%)	30%	
PUP adjustment	1,200	

The unrealised element of the profit from sales between an associate and a parent is the parent's share of the total profit from goods left in the group.

The profit needs to be time-apportioned for the six months of ownership, with the $15,000 impairment then deducted.

Share of profit of associate = 30% × $300,000 ($600,000 × 6/12) - $1,200 - $15,000 = **$73,800**

112 B

The investment in associate is calculated as

		$
Cost of investment	[(20% × 1,000,000)/4] × $4.5	225,000
P% × A's post acquisition movement in net assets less	(20% × ($4,600,000 – $5,000,000)	(80,000)
Impairment		(100,000)
PUP (when P sells to A)		(10,000)
		35,000

Dolph own 20% of Chuck's shares, therefore Dolph has bought 200,000 shares (20% of Chuck's 1,000,000 shares).

As Dolph issued 1 share for every 4 purchased, Dolph issued 50,000 new shares to acquire Chuck. These had a market value of $4.50 and were worth $225,000.

Dolph must include 20% of Chuck's post-acquisition movement in net assets. Chuck has made a post-acquisition loss of $400,000 (net assets at acquisition were $5,000,000 [share capital $1,000,000 + retained earnings $4,000,000] and net assets at 31 December 20X8 were $4,600,000).

Post- acquisition loss = $4,600,000 – $5,000,000 = $400,000 loss.

The impairment in Chuck of $100,000 must be removed from the value of the investment in the associate.

The PUP adjustment when Dolph (parent) sells to Chuck (associate) is calculated as P% of inter group profit on goods left in the group = 20% × $50,000 = $10,000. This is removed from the investment in associate when P sells to A.

COMPLEX GROUPS (INDIRECT HOLDINGS)

113 $44M

	$m
Goodwill in acquisition of C:	
Consideration paid by B	480
Less indirect holding adjustment: 480 × 20%	(96)
Consideration effectively incurred by AZ	384
Fair value of NCI at acquisition	280
Less fair value of net assets at acquisition	(620)
	44

SUBJECT F2 : ADVANCED FINANCIAL REPORTING

114 B, D

AQ controls B and B controls C. Therefore AQ indirectly controls C and it should be recognised as a subsidiary. Therefore A is incorrect.

AQ does not gain control of C until it acquires its shareholding in B on 1 January 20X3. Therefore C is incorrect.

AQ's effective holding in C is 48% (80% × 60%) and it is this percentage of C's post-acquisition retained earnings that would be included within consolidated reserves. Therefore E is incorrect.

115 C

	D	M
NCI share of profit:	$	$
Subsidiary profit for the year	87,000	70,000
Less: inter-group investment income (60% × 20,000)	(12,000)	
	75,000	
NCI share	× 25%	× 55%
	18,750	38,500

BV's effective holding in M = 75% × 60% = 45% therefore NCI = 55%

Total profit attributable to NCI = 18,750 + 38,500 = $57,250

116 $1,080,000

Post-acquisition reserves of CA:	$000
Reserves at reporting date	8,000
Less reserves at acquisition (FG gained control on 1.1.X5)	(5,600)
	2,400
Group share 75% × 60%	× 45%
	1,080

117 C

60% of EF's shares are held within the AB group making EF is a subsidiary. Therefore A and B are incorrect.

An indirect holding adjustment would be applied to the consideration paid by CD, but this would be based on AB's NCI share in CD which is 40%. Therefore D is incorrect.

The effective holding of AB in EF = 30% + (60% × 30%) = 48%, making C the correct answer.

ANSWERS TO OBJECTIVE TEST QUESTIONS : SECTION 2

118 C

	$
Non-controlling interest in ST:	
Fair value of NCI at acquisition	300,000
NCI share of post-acquisition reserves	
48% × (580,000 – 275,000)	146,400
	446,400

XZ's effective holding in ST = 80% × 65% = 52%, therefore NCI = 48%.

Tutorial note:

When calculating goodwill arising on the acquisition of ST, an indirect holding adjustment of $90,000 (20% × $450,000) would be deducted and this amount would also be deducted from non-controlling interests. However, it relates to WV's NCI (20%) rather than ST's NCI and therefore does not form part of the above calculation.

119 C

	$
Goodwill in TW:	
Consideration paid by SD	35,000
Less indirect holding adjustment (20% × 35,000)	(7,000)
PB' share of consideration paid (80% × 35,000)	28,000
Fair value of NCI at acquisition	31,000
Less fair value of net assets acquired	(36,400)
	22,600

120 B, D

FG is a subsidiary, as DG controls LM and LM controls FG giving DG indirect control of FG. Therefore B is incorrect (and A is correct).

DG's effective holding in FG = 60% × 60% = 36% therefore NCI = 64% and C is correct.

Only DG's share of the consideration paid by LM for the shares in FG should be reflected in the goodwill calculation. DG owns 60% of LM and therefore this is the share of consideration paid that should be included. Therefore D is incorrect (and E is correct).

CHANGES IN GROUP STRUCTURE

121 The gain or loss on disposal recognised in the consolidated statement of profit or loss on disposal of the shares in SD on 1 October 20x8 will be calculated as follows:

Gain or loss on disposal	$000
Sale proceeds	2,500
Fair value of remaining holding	**1,200**
Net assets at disposal	(3,300)
Goodwill at disposal	(480)
NCI at disposal	**740**
Gain/(loss) on disposal	**660**

	$000
NCI at disposal:	
Fair value of NCI at acquisition	680
NCI share of post-acquisition reserves	
20% × (1,300,000 – 1,000,000)	60
	740

Tutorial note:

As the net assets and goodwill at disposal are shown as negative figures, the NCI should be shown as positive. This results in an overall gain on disposal of $660,000.

122 C

The reduction in the NCI will be 15/25 = 60% of the balance on the reserve prior to the acquisition of additional shares.

ANSWERS TO OBJECTIVE TEST QUESTIONS : SECTION 2

123 Extract from the consolidated statement of changes in equity for RBE group for the year ended 31 December 20X1

	Attributable to equity holders of parent	Attributable to non-controlling interest
	$000	$000
Balance at start of year	3,350	650
Comprehensive income for the year	1,280	150
Dividends paid	(200)	**(30)**
Adjustment to NCI for additional purchase of DCA shares	**BLANK**	**(503)**
Adjustment to parent's equity for additional purchase of DCA shares	**(37)**	**BLANK**

Dividends paid to NCI = 100,000 × 30% (NCI share in April 20X1)

Reduction in NCI = 755,000 × 20/30 = 503,333

The adjustment to parent's equity = 503,333 − 540,000 = (36,667)

124 **$136,000**

Adjustment to equity reserves:	$
Cash received	400,000
Less amount transferred to NCI	
30% × (800,000 net assets + 80,000 goodwill)	(264,000)
	136,000

125 **D**

NCI at date of transfer:	$000
Fair value of NCI at acquisition	1,960
NCI share of post-acquisition reserves	
40% × (3,240 − 2,760)	192
	2,152

Proportionate reduction in NCI (debit) = 20/40 × 2,152,000 = 1,076,000

Adjustment through equity reserves = 1,076,000 − 1,000,000 = 76,000

SUBJECT F2 : ADVANCED FINANCIAL REPORTING

126 **$327,000**

	$000	$000
Sale proceeds		960
Fair value of retained interest		792
Less carrying amount of subsidiary at disposal:		
Net assets (100,000 + 1,800,000)	1,900	
Goodwill (fully impaired)	–	
NCI (25% × 1,900,000)	(475)	
		(1,425)
Gain on disposal		327

127 **A**

	$000
Adjustment to equity reserves:	
Decrease in NCI 10/30 × 3,030,000	1,010
Less cash paid	(1,172)
Negative adjustment = debit	(162)

128 **D, E**

Goodwill is only recognised once, when control is achieved, therefore **A is incorrect**.

On the 1 April 20X2, a step-acquisition from 15% to 75% occurred. This is a step-acquisition that achieves control. The 15% is treated as if it is disposed by revaluing to fair value and gains or losses recognised in the profit or loss account. At this date, ROB has applied the accounting treatment of a FVOCI financial asset and, as a result, the gains of $200,000 ($800,000 - $600,000) are already recorded in reserves. As per IFRS 9, upon disposal of an equity financial asset that is classified as FVOCI, any gains or losses held in reserves will NOT be reclassified to profit or loss. On 1 April 20X2, the gains shown in profit or loss are nil. Therefore, **B is incorrect**.

The goodwill should reflect the acquisition of a 75% subsidiary, therefore **C is incorrect** and **E is correct**.

The gains on re-measurement to fair value should be reversed out upon consolidation as the investment is treated as a subsidiary rather than FVOCI. The total gain recorded in ROB's FVOCI reserve to be reversed on consolidation will be:

	$
Fair value of 75%	4,000,000
Cost of 60%	(2,900,000)
Cost of 15%	(600,000)
Total gain recorded in reserves on FVOCI assets by 30 September 20X2	500,000

Option D is correct

ANSWERS TO OBJECTIVE TEST QUESTIONS : SECTION 2

129 A

Goodwill would include the cost of the shares just acquired and the fair value of the previous shareholding (rather than its original cost). Therefore B is incorrect.

Control is achieved by PT on 1 October 20X5 and therefore this is an acquisition of a subsidiary rather than a transfer between owners (which would relate to an existing subsidiary). Therefore C is incorrect.

The consolidated statement of financial position reflects the position at the reporting date, at which point the investment is a subsidiary. Therefore D is incorrect.

130 B

Impact in profit or loss:	$m
Deemed proceeds (= fair value)	390
Less carrying amount of associate at disposal	
270 cost + (40% × (800 – 600))	(350)
Gain on disposal of associate	40

131 B, C, D

BH's total shareholding after the acquisition on 1 June 20X1 is 55% therefore BH has control, rather than significant influence. Therefore A is incorrect.

NJ should be consolidated as a subsidiary from 1 June 20X1, therefore E is incorrect.

132 D

Goodwill in CD:	$000
Consideration paid for 60% holding	5,175
Fair value of previous 10% holding	1,000
	6,175
Fair value of NCI at acquisition	2,700
Less fair value of net assets acquired	(6,500)
	2,375

133 A

Profit attributable to NCI:	$
Subsidiary profit (post-acquisition) = 220,000 × 9/12	165,000
NCI share	× 25%
	41,250

ST is an associate until 1 April 20X5, when it becomes a subsidiary. Therefore the profit attributable to NCI only relates to 9 months of the year.

SUBJECT F2 : ADVANCED FINANCIAL REPORTING

134 A, B, F

The sale of shares results in control being lost. The subsidiary should be derecognised in full and the fair value of the remaining holding recognised as a financial asset.

C is incorrect, as the fair value of the remaining holding is added to sale proceeds and then 100% of the carrying amount of the subsidiary is deducted from the resulting figure.

D is incorrect as there will be no remaining goodwill once control has been lost.

E is incorrect as the NCI should be derecognised in full.

135 B, C, F

ST still controls UV and therefore should continue to consolidate 100% of the assets and liabilities. Therefore A is incorrect (and B and C are correct).

There will be profit attributable to the NCI for the full year although the percentage changes after 9 months. Therefore D is incorrect.

On disposal of the shares, the NCI will increase and therefore is credited. Therefore E is incorrect (and F is correct).

CONSOLIDATED CASH FLOW STATEMENTS

136 D, E, F

Items A, B and C would all appear within the investing activities section.

137 A, C

Items B, D and E would all appear within the operating activities section.

138 A

Movement in inventory	$000
Balance b/f	36,000
Disposal of subsidiary	(3,600)
	32,400
Increase in inventory (balancing figure)	2,400
Balance c/f	34,800

An increase in inventory is shown as a **negative** adjustment to profit in the operating activities section of the statement of cash flows.

139 $3,800,000

Movement in PPE:	$000
Balance b/f	15,600
Depreciation	(1,800)
Disposal of subsidiary	(800)
	13,000
Purchase of PPE (balancing figure = cash paid)	3,800
Balance c/f	16,800

140 C

Movement in NCI:	$000
Balance b/f	18,300
NCI share of total comprehensive income	680
Acquisition of subsidiary 30% × 4,400	1,320
	20,300
Dividends paid to NCI (balancing figure)	(800)
Balance c/f	19,500

141 $2,130,000

Movement in retained earnings:	$000
Balance b/f	20,100
Profit attributable to parent shareholders	3,880
	23,980
Dividends paid to parent shareholders (balancing figure)	(2,130)
Balance c/f	21,850

142 B

Movement in investment in associate:	$000
Balance b/f	5,700
Share of associate profit for the year	1,800
Share of associate other comprehensive income for the year	200
	7,700
Dividends received from associate (cash inflow = bal figure)	(1,500)
Balance c/f	6,200

143 A

Movement in goodwill:	$000
Balance b/f	7,200
Acquisition of subsidiary (see below)	1,370
	8,570
Impairment (balancing figure)	(570)
Balance c/f	8,000

Goodwill arising on acquisition of subsidiary:

	$000
Cash consideration	500
Shares consideration 1,000 × 3.95	3,950
Value of NCI 30% × 4,400	1,320
Less fair value of net assets acquired	(4,400)
	1,370

FOREIGN CURRENCY CONSOLIDATIONS

144 B, E

The exchange difference arising on translation of a foreign operation is recognised in other comprehensive income, therefore A is incorrect.

There is no requirement for subsidiaries to present their financial statements in the presentation currency of the parent although they may choose to do so, therefore C is incorrect.

The exchange difference on goodwill is only allocated between parent shareholders and non-controlling interest if the non-controlling interest is measured at fair value at the date of acquisition. Therefore D is incorrect.

145 $9,409

	Crowns
Consideration paid	204,000
Less fair value of net assets at acquisition	
(1,000 + 180,000)	(181,000)
Goodwill at acquisition	23,000
Less impairment (10%)	(2,300)
Goodwill at the reporting date	20,700

Goodwill at reporting date translated at closing rate = 20,700/2.2 = $9,409

ANSWERS TO OBJECTIVE TEST QUESTIONS : SECTION 2

146 C

	A$
NCI share of total comprehensive income:	
Subsidiary's profit translated at average rate = 800,000/2.1	380,952
Exchange loss on net assets	(50,000)
	330,952
NCI share	× 20%
	66,190

Exchange loss on goodwill is fully attributable to parent shareholders, as non-controlling interest is measured at acquisition using the proportionate method.

147 Exchange difference on net assets for the year:

Exchange difference on net assets		$
Closing net assets at	**Closing rate**	X
Less: comprehensive income at	**Average rate for the year**	(X)
Less: opening net assets	**Opening rate**	(X)
Exchange difference on net assets for the year		X

148 $54,000

	Crowns 000	Exchange rate	$000
Consideration paid	13,984		
Fair value of NCI	3,496		
Less fair value of net assets acquired	(15,800)		
Goodwill at acquisition	1,680	/ 1.61	1,043
Less impairment (20% × 1,680)	(336)	/ 1.58	(213)
Exchange difference (balancing figure)			54
Goodwill at the reporting date	1,344	/ 1.52	884

149 C

	Dinar 000	Exchange rate	$
Net assets at start of year (3,800 – 1,350)	2,450	/ 36	68,056
Comprehensive income for year	1,350	/ 35	38,571
			106,627
Exchange difference (balancing figure)			12,123
Net assets at reporting date	3,800	/ 32	118,750

150 B

	B$000
Consideration paid (5,200 × 0.50)	2,600
Fair value of NCI	600
Less fair value of net assets acquired	(2,800)
Goodwill at acquisition and reporting date	400

Goodwill at reporting date translated at closing rate = 400,000/0.71 = A$563,380

151 B

Property, plant and equipment	Gr	$
GD		12,800,000
WR:		
Book value	4,300,000	
Fair value adjustment	500,000	
Fair value depreciation 500 × 3/40	(37,500)	
	4,762,500 /4.1	1,161,585
		13,961,585

152 B, D

A is incorrect. As per IAS 21 *The effects of changes in foreign exchange rates*, the functional currency of NJ is the currency of the primary economic environment in which it operates and is therefore set at individual entity level. Therefore A is incorrect (and B is correct).

C is incorrect. Sales prices/revenue is only one of the factors to be considered in determining the functional currency and this can be outweighed by other factors, as is the case here. As NJ's costs are incurred in the Kron, it operates autonomously and raises finance in the Kron, this should be its functional currency (therefore D is correct).

The directors of NJ can choose the presentation currency. It does not have to be the functional currency and therefore E is incorrect.

ANALYSIS OF FINANCIAL PERFORMANCE AND POSITION

153 75.4%

Debt:	$m
Long-term borrowings	400
Redeemable preference shares	100
	500

Gearing ratio = debt/equity = 500/663 × 100 = 75.4%

154 17.3

Profit before interest and tax (PBIT) = 179 + 11 = 190

Interest cover = PBIT/finance costs = 190/11 = 17.3

155 37.4%

Profit before interest and tax (excluding associate) = 268 – 55 = 213

Capital employed (excluding associate) = equity + debt – investment in associate

= 465 + 190 – 86 = 569

Return on capital employed = 213/569 × 100 = 37.4%

156 C

A is incorrect. A significant investment in PPE shortly before the year end would result in a large increase in capital employed with little effect in profit.

B is incorrect. A revaluation of land and buildings will increase capital employed (revaluation reserve is part of equity) but will have no positive effect on profit.

C is correct. The impact on capital employed would be in the previous period and therefore in the current year's ratio the improvement in profitability would be reflected.

D is incorrect. An issue of shares to repay long-term borrowings would have no effect on capital employed (as both equity and debt are included in the calculation). There would be a saving in finance costs, however the profit used in the ROCE calculation does not include finance costs and therefore the ratio would not be affected.

157 B, C, D

A is possibly true however the fall in retained earnings could also be caused by a significant dividend payment.

E is possibly true however the increase in long-term borrowings could arise from amortisation of the liability rather than additional borrowings.

158 C

There are various ways that gearing can be calculated, so to be comparable we firstly need to figure out the method used for entity B.

Gearing of entity B = 5.9% and equity = 3,403.

Therefore, the figures used for the numerator must be 5.9% × 3,403 = 200.8

Looking at B's figures, it appears that only long-term borrowings have been included in the calculation (200/3,403 = 5.9%)

Therefore the comparable gearing ratio for A = 1,000/3,754 = 26.6%

159 B

A is incorrect. A's revenue is significantly lower than B's and therefore B is more likely to be benefiting from economies of scale.

B is correct, as follows:

	A $m		B $m
Gross profit = 26% × $160m	41.6	Gross profit = 17% × $300m	51
Operating profit = 9% × $160m	14.4	Operating profit = 11% × $300m	33
Operating expenses	27.2		18

C is incorrect. A has higher gearing than B and would therefore be considered a higher risk by lenders. (The low interest rate may however explain why A are using debt finance in the first place.)

D is incorrect. LOP's gross profit margin is higher than both A's and B's and therefore acquisition of either entity is likely to reduce the overall margin of the combined business (unless cost savings can be achieved as a result of the acquisition).

160 A

B is incorrect. A has higher gearing than B and therefore reduced capacity for additional borrowings.

C is incorrect. Gross profit margins increase with operating profit margins decreases would suggest that A has high operating expenses. It does not prove any creative accounting or unethical behaviour on behalf of the directors of A.

D is incorrect. A's lower operating profit margin does not indicate that B operates in the budget sector of the market. A's higher gross profit margin could suggest that it can charge higher prices than B. Its lower operating margin suggests higher costs. This could be caused by higher rentals as a result of operating out of more prestigious locations than B. It would appear more likely that B would be the budget operator.

161 B

Different tax rates would affect any comparison of the profit after tax margin, but has no effect on profit from operations and therefore the profit from operations margin.

162 B

Profit margins:	20X9		20X8	
Gross = 372/1,430	26%	Gross = 317/1,022	31%
Operating = 130/1,430	9%	Operating = 155/1,022	15%

Both gross and operating profit margins have fallen, therefore A and D are correct.

The increase in distribution costs is 68% compared to an increase in revenue of 40%, therefore B is incorrect and C is correct.

ANSWERS TO OBJECTIVE TEST QUESTIONS : SECTION 2

163 A

A's revenue is similar, and slightly lower, than B's so economies of scale is not a valid explanation of the difference in gross profit margins.

164 B, D, E

A potential minority shareholder would not have access to the information suggested in A or C.

The other information would be readily available.

165 D

An increase in the payables payment period should improve the cash position, as the entity is delaying cash outflows. (It may be a consequence of a lack of cash, but not the reason for it.)

166 B

A is incorrect as a significant outflow in investing activities suggest growth.

C is incorrect. It is not a certainty that QW has made a profit, it could have significant non-cash items in expenses that, when added back, reconcile a loss to a cash inflow.

D is incorrect as QW still have positive cash and cash equivalents of $590m at the year end.

167 B

Gearing is calculated as debt/equity or debt/debt + equity. If an item of property plant and equipment is revalued during a period, an increase in revaluation reserve would arise. This is the case for EE.

The increase in revaluation will cause the equity to increase. In turn, the gearing will be expected to reduce.

Gearing 20X1 = 585/1,593 = 36.7%

Gearing 20X2 = 553/1,437 = 38.5%

"EE must have made a loss in the year as retained earnings have fallen" is not true. The fall in retained earnings could also be caused by a significant dividend payment, not necessarily because EE is loss making.

Bonus issues in shares are free issues of shares. They would cause an increase in share capital. No cash is received from these shares. No increase in share premium would arise. As share premium as increased as well as share capital, new shares must have been issued during the year for cash in excess of the nominal value of the shares.

"EE must have secured additional long-term borrowings of $25m" is not necessarily true. The increase in long-term borrowings could arise from amortisation of the liability rather than additional borrowings.

168 C,E

The following statements are not realistic expectations:

"VB has recorded significant gains on the change in fair value of its FVOCI investments" is not a realistic explanation as this would decrease gearing. There would be an increase in VB's equity caused by an increase in the FVOCI reserve. VB would be expected to have a lower gearing than JK.

"VB's management is better at controlling costs than JK's" is not a valid explanation. VB would be expected to have higher profits, thus higher retained earnings in equity and lower gearing.

"VB has reduced its effective tax rate by employing tax accountants" is not a realistic explanation. The fees for the tax accountants and the tax benefit are held in profits. This would increase VB's profits in comparison to JK (assuming the benefits of using the accountant outweigh the costs). This would increase retained earnings in equity causing a reduction to gearing.

169 A, D, E

B is incorrect. The gross profit margin for retail operations in 20X2 is 30.0% (1,200/4,004) compared with 29.6% (1,095/3,700) last year.

C is incorrect. The shop overheads would affect operating profit and profit before tax margins, but not the gross profit margin.

F is incorrect. The online store has a higher profit before tax margin (138/1,096 = 12.6%) than the hotel contract (82/900 = 9.1%).

170 0.4 TIMES

Dividend cover = Profit for the year/Dividend paid

$750,000/(3,750,000 × 0.5) = $750,000/1,875,000

171 A, B, E

Non-current asset turnover = Revenue/NCAs.

C is incorrect. A revaluation of non-current assets would reduce non-current asset turnover and therefore result in A's being lower than B's.

D is incorrect. A manufacturing entity would have a higher level of NCAs and therefore a lower NCA turnover than a service entity.

172 A, B, E

C and D would be considered limitations to users rather than benefits (although C could be argued to be a benefit to the preparers, i.e. the directors).

The flexibility in defining reporting segments means that directors have the ability to manipulate the results.

There will be a lack of comparability between entities as the reportable segments are unlikely to be defined in the same way.

ANSWERS TO OBJECTIVE TEST QUESTIONS : **SECTION 2**

173 D

The increase in shares will reduce gearing. Equity will increase on the exercise of the options as cash is received by the company (the exercise price), the equity balance built up over the vesting period is removed and is replace by share capital and share premium. As the increase in share capital and share premium will outweigh the removal of the shared based payment equity balance, equity within the gearing calculation will increase. Gearing will decrease. Therefore D is correct.

There would be a dilution to earnings per share as the number of shares would increase and there would be no effect on profit. Therefore A and C are incorrect.

The issue of new shares is likely to affect the share price and therefore B is incorrect.

174 Formula for dividend cover:

Dividend cover
Net profit for the year
Dividend paid during the year

175 C

Interest cover is not affected as no time has elapsed during 20X6 for the finance costs to accrue. C is incorrect.

Current ratio considers current assets vs current liabilities. Acquisitions of plant and machinery and bank loans are considered non-current assets and liabilities. Current ratio is not impacted by the transaction.

Gearing would be expected to increase as a result of the higher levels of debt.

ROCE would be expected to reduce as operating profits would be unaffected and capital employed would increase. No time exists during the year ended March 20X6 for any discernible benefit to arise from the investment in the PPE. It would be reasonable to assume that profits are unaffected. The capital employed would increase as a result of the new long term financing.

176 A, C, D

Profit is not affected as the land is non-depreciable and the revaluation surplus would be credited to other comprehensive income rather than profit. Therefore B is incorrect.

The current ratio only includes current assets (and liabilities) and therefore E is incorrect.

177 D

A is not valid. The increase in the long-term borrowings is from amortising the liability element of the convertible bonds rather than raising additional finance.

B is not valid. Increased finance costs would not be reflected in the return on capital employed as the profit used in the calculation is before deduction of finance costs.

C is not valid. Both gross profit margin and profit before tax margin have increased therefore it would be highly unlikely (although not impossible!) that the operating margin would have fallen.

SUBJECT F2 : ADVANCED FINANCIAL REPORTING

178 **1.54**

Capital employed = 1,300 + 258 = 1,558

Therefore asset turnover = 2,400/1,558 = 1.54

179 **A**

A is not a limitation when comparing a single entity from one period to the next. If an entity changes an accounting policy it is required to restate its comparatives to reflect the new policy and therefore comparison will still be made on a like for like basis.

Tutorial note:

This would be a limitation when comparing ratios of two different entities.

180 **D**

Return on capital employed (ROCE) can be calculated either with or without the associate, as long as the numerator and denominator are consistent.

We therefore need to firstly consider which method has been used for the calculation of B's ROCE.

With associate included, B's ROCE = (509 + 32)/(1,500 + 650) = 25.2%

With associate excluded, B's ROCE = (509 + 32 – 25)/(1,500 + 650 – 350) = 28.7%

Therefore, the comparable ROCE for A would exclude the associate.

Comparable ROCE for A = (680 + 25 – 148)/(950 + 500 – 570) = 63.3%

181 **A reduction, a reduction, an increase**

When assessing reasons for changes in cash and cash equivalents **a reduction** in inventory, **a reduction** in receivables and **an increase** in payables would all explain an improvement in the cash position.

182 **A, B, F**

LW are unlikely to have increased selling prices when there has been no growth in sales volume for the past five years, therefore C is not a realistic conclusion.

An increase in payables payment period would improve rather than worsen the cash position therefore D is not a realistic conclusion.

The quick ratio does not include inventory and therefore E is not a realistic conclusion.

183 **A, B**

Breakdown of operating expenses and cash flow forecasts are internal information and therefore these would not be readily available.

Industry statistics are available for most industries.

Interim financial statements and operating and financial reviews are typically published by listed entities.

Tutorial note:

RB could approach the directors of LW to try and access the internal information. In practice, how likely this is to be successful would depend on whether LW are keen for RB to acquire the entity.

184

Return on capital employed	Gross profit margin
$\dfrac{\text{Revenue} - \text{cost of sales} - \text{operating expenses}}{\text{Capital employed}}$	$\dfrac{\text{Revenue} - \text{cost of sales}}{\text{Revenue}}$

185 B

Dividend cover = Profit for the year/Dividend paid

It would therefore not be distorted by any incomparability of share prices.

186 B, C, D

A, E and F are all examples of information not typically published by listed entities. It would be highly unlikely that a minority shareholder would be able to obtain copies of these.

187 C

C suggests that X's cost of sales would be relatively higher than Y and this would result in X's gross profit margin being lower rather than higher.

188 B

A revaluation policy would reduce gearing rather than increase it.

189 MORE, X, Y

If further debt finance was required by the new companies, debt finance would be more likely to be obtained for Y.

Based upon the gearing levels of the two entities, an investment in X would appear to be riskier than an investment in Y.

190 A, C

Although the current and quick ratios have both reduced, they are still at very comfortable levels and therefore liquidity is not a significant concern.

Inventory is not included in the quick ratio and therefore would not be the reason for a change in it.

Tutorial note:

Over-trading occurs when there is significant growth and a failure to support the growth with long-term finance. It will typically result in an increase in working capital ratios and a reduction in operating cash flows.

191 B

The increase in equity and capital employed would result in a reduction on both ratios.

192 A, B, C, D, E, F

All information is likely to be accessible, as the lender can simply turn down the application for finance if the entity does not provide it.

193 Higher, despite

A is incurring significantly **higher** operating expenses than B. Its return on capital employed is higher than B's **despite** the revaluation of non-current assets in the year.

A revaluation will have a negative effect on ROCE. The operating expenses can actually be calculated from the information provided (although this would not be necessary to answer the question).

	A $000		B $000
Gross profit = 36% × $5.7m	2,052	Gross profit = 31% × $5.3m	1,643
Operating expenses (bal fig)	(1,276)	Operating expenses (bal fig)	(796)
Finance costs	(120)	Finance costs	(105)
PBT = 11.5% × $5.7m	656	PBT = 14% × $5.3m	742

194 D

D is incorrect.

A has a lower level of debt but a higher finance cost. This would suggest that either A has repaid borrowings part way through the year (its average borrowings are higher than at the year-end) or B has increased its borrowings during the year (and its finance costs therefore do not reflect a full year's worth of interest).

ANSWERS TO OBJECTIVE TEST QUESTIONS : SECTION 2

195 B, C, E, F

A is comparable, as the costs of depreciating the computer equipment and the finance costs on the debt for A Ltd and the rental expenses for the short term lease of B Ltd would be charged through administrative expenses. This would leave gross profit margins unaffected.

D is comparable as the current ratio reflects working capital balances and these would not be directly affected by the method of finance used for the acquisitions.

The other ratios are all affected by debt or finance costs. A Ltd buys the assets with debt finance, whilst B Ltd finances the computer equipment through low value leases which do not create a lease liability. The ratios which use finance costs and debt are deemed distorted for direct comparison.

196 B

A is not a valid conclusion. The fall in retained earnings could also have been due to a significant dividend payment.

C is not a valid conclusion. The reduction in share premium matches the increase in share capital, suggesting that the issue of shares was a bonus issue which does not raise finance.

D is not a valid conclusion. The increase in borrowings could be amortisation of the existing borrowings rather than additional borrowings being taken out.

197 Investing, financing

When analysing a statement of cash flows, a cash outflow from **investing** activities would suggest that the entity is expanding its operations.

An outflow from investing activities is often matched with an inflow from **financing** activities as long term finance should be used to finance investment.

198 A reduction in selling prices

Given the circumstances that TYU finds itself in, the most likely reason for the reduction in gross profit margin is **a reduction in selling prices**.

This would be the most obvious response to the new entrant to maintain or regain market share. Revenue has not fallen which suggests that this has been a successful move.

199 C

A is not a valid conclusion. An increase in inventory holding period would increase the current ratio (as inventory would be higher).

B is not a valid conclusion. Inventory is excluded from the quick ratio calculation.

D is not a valid conclusion. An increase in inventory at the reporting date would reduce cost of sales (as closing inventory is deducted from this figure) and therefore increase the gross profit margin.

200 A

Although the current ratio is greater than 1, the quick ratio is only 0.5 and therefore TYU is facing significant liquidity concerns. The inventory is not a liquid asset (with a holding period of 167 days) and therefore the quick ratio provides a better measure of liquidity than the current ratio.

The current ratio is likely to only be greater than 1 because of the significant inventory holding.

201 A, B, D, E, F

The measurement of non-controlling interest only affects the calculation of goodwill and the NCI share of equity. Any goodwill impairment would be charged to operating expenses rather than cost of sales so there would be no effect on gross profit.

All of the other differences could affect the calculation of gross profit.

A revaluation of non-current assets will affect the amount of depreciation being charged to profit or loss. If the assets are production related then depreciation should be charged through cost of sales.

202 C

EBITDA represents earnings before interest, tax, depreciation and amortisation. Earnings is calculated as earnings attributable to ordinary shareholders = PAT – NCI share of profit – irredeemable preference dividends. As no tax is given in the information, earnings can be approximated to be profit before tax (PBT).

	$000
PBT	224
Add back	
Finance cost	15
Depreciation (15 + 5)	20
Amortisation	12
EBITDA	271

The fuel costs and staff salaries are normal operating expenses that should be included as an expense within earnings.

RANDOM QUESTION TESTS

RANDOM QUESTION TEST 1

1.1 C

Cash-settled share-based payments will create a liability over the vesting period. No equity balances will arise. Only equity-settled share-based payments cause increases to equity within the SOFP. Option C suggests all share-based payments will create equity balances. This is incorrect.

1.2 B

The bonds are a financial liability as they contain an obligation (to pay interest at the coupon rate of 5% and to repay at a premium of 10% after five years).

The bonds are not a financial asset. The bonds have been issued. This means the business is selling the bonds to raise finance. A financial liability is created.

The initial recognition would be at a value of $2,975,000 ($3m less the issue costs of $25,000).

In addition to the coupon payments of 5% each year, there are additional finance costs: the issue costs and the redemption premium. The effective rate of interest will therefore be greater than 5%.

The liability is shown at amortised cost over the five years and the carrying amount of the bond will therefore change at each reporting date. The carrying amount is given as:

B/f	Interest at effective interest rate	Payment at coupon rate	C/f
x	x	(x)	x

After 5 years the carrying amount should be $3,300,000 as this is the amount due for repayment on the redemption date. At each year end, however, the amortised cost will be a different value (lower than the $3,300,000).

1.3 26%

$k_d = i(1-T)/ P_o$

$(k_d \times P_o)/i = 1-T$

$T = 1 - ((k_d \times P_o)/i)$

$T = 1-[(0.0976 \times 91)/12]$

$T = 26\%$

1.4 A

NCI % × S's PAT = 20% × $600k	$120k
NCI% × PURP (S selling to P) = 20% × 60k	($12k)
NCI% × Impairment (NCI at FV) = 20% × $100k	($10k)
Total NCI = $120k - $12k - $10k	**$98k**

SUBJECT F2 : ADVANCED FINANCIAL REPORTING

1.5 B

The quick ratio is made up of the current assets excluding inventory divided by the current liabilities. In the case of Couts Ltd, this will be receivables and cash divided by payables and the overdraft.

($120,000 + $15,000)/($105,000+$51,000) = 0.87:1.

1.6 B

A new share issue would increase the level of equity. This would therefore decrease the level of gearing.

Revaluation losses would either reduce revaluation reserve (if the asset had been previously revalued upwards) or profits. Either way, equity would reduce (any impact to profits would reduce retained earnings). Consequently, gearing would increase.

New loans increase debt and, therefore, gearing.

Assets under leases would create a lease liability. Hence, gearing would increase.

1.7 A, D

EMI group consists of a 75% sub, LI and an indirectly controlled sub-subsidiary, A. EMI will consolidate A using an effective shareholding of 75% × 65% = 48.75%.

As A is an indirectly controlled sub-sub, an indirect holding adjustment (IHA) will be required to reflect the element of the investment in A contributed by shareholders outside of the EMI group (the NCI's of LI). The indirect holding adjustment in the goodwill of A will be calculated as NCI % in LI × cost of investment = 25% × $4m = $1m. Option A is correct.

Sub-subs are consolidated from the date of effective control. This is the later of the date that the parent acquires the sub or the date that the sub acquires the sub-sub. Therefore, the effective date of control for A is 31st July 20X9, not 31st Dec 20X8. Goodwill will include the fair value of the net assets of A as at 31st July 20X9, not the 31st Dec 20X8. Option B is not correct.

LI is a directly owned subsidiary. Therefore, no IHA adjustments are relevant. Option C is not correct.

As the sub, LI, is 75% owned by the parent, EMI, 75% of the post-acquisition profits of LI are taken to group retained earnings. Option D is correct.

Group retained earnings will include 48.75% of the sub-sub's (A's) post-acquisition profits, not 65%. Option E is not correct.

1.8 B

Total revenue = 65% × $12m = $7.8m.

The amount to be recorded in year 2 will be $7.8m less the amounts recorded in year 1.

Revenue recorded in year 2 = 7.8m – 3.25m = $4.55m.

ANSWERS TO OBJECTIVE TEST QUESTIONS : SECTION 2

1.9 D

Intra group outstanding balances must be eliminated from consolidation. Elimination will only occur once the outstanding balances (payables and receivables) agree,

In this case, the sub (RAT) has despatched goods to the parent, (SHA) prior to the year-end which have not been received by the parent. The goods are in transit at the year end.

Before elimination of the intra group outstanding balances can occur, the goods in transit must be recorded as if they were delivered before the year end.

Dr Inventory $2.5m Cr Payables $2.5m.

SHA had $45m owing to RAT before this transaction was recorded. Therefore, $47.5m is now shown as outstanding to RAT after the effects of the above entry. Assuming no other items are in transit, this means that RAT must have a receivable of $47.5m.

To eliminate the intragroup outstanding, Dr payables $47.5m Cr receivables $47.5m.

The overall result is:

Dr inventory $2.5m (increasing inventory)

Dr Payables $45m (decreasing payables)

Cr Receivables $47.5m (decreasing receivables)

1.10 A, C, F

Option B states that Y is paying their suppliers on time. Y is actually paying its suppliers earlier than is required, which means it is not maximising the advantages of this cheap source of finance. This could be beneficial if it is taking advantage of settlement discounts. There are no settlement discounts available. Therefore, Y would be better served taking further advantage of the credit available from their suppliers.

Z should not exceed the payment terms offered to it by suppliers. As such, it is not being managed in the best manner. If Z's suppliers do not get paid on time, they may not deliver raw materials when needed. This would interrupt Z's production and may lead to stockouts. The supplier could even force Z into liquidation if the failure to pay what is owed continues.

We cannot conclude whether Y requires a bank overdraft from the information provided.

RANDOM QUESTION TEST 2

2.1 C

Deferred tax arises due to temporary differences between the carrying amount and the tax base. The carrying amount of the provision is a $1m liability. This causes the carrying amount to be lower than the tax base. This will create a deferred tax asset within the financial statements. Suarez will get tax relief when paying the costs associated with the damages. This tax relief creates a deferred tax asset.

Therefore, to record an increase in a deferred tax asset, a debit will be posted to the deferred tax asset/liability account.

The deferred tax ASSET, not liability will have a value of $1m × 25% = $250k as at the year ended 31st Dec 20X5. A is incorrect.

The movement in the deferred tax asset is $125k (DT asset at y/e 31st Dec 20X5 - DT asset at y/e 31st Dec 20X4 = [$1m × 25%] - [500k × 25%] = $250k - $125k = $125k. This movement is taken to profit or loss NOT reserves. This is to ensure the tax impact is matched against the accounting treatment of the provision. B is incorrect.

The temporary difference is calculated as the Carrying amount - Tax Base = $1m – 0 = $1m. The tax base of a liability is given as CV – amounts written off in future tax computations. For y/e 20X5, the CV is $1m, the tax base = 0 ($1m -$1m). The temporary difference is $1m, not $500k. D is incorrect.

2.2 B

The correct statement is "Upon liquidation of a company, the shareholders will receive a pay-out after all other finance providers have been paid". Ordinary shareholders are subordinate to all other finance providers so they will receive their pay-out last.

Dividends are paid at the discretion of the directors.

Dividends are a distribution of earnings and paid out of post-tax profits. Dividends paid are represented in the financial statements through retained earnings, rather than in the profit or loss account.

The ordinary shareholders have voting rights.

ANSWERS TO OBJECTIVE TEST QUESTIONS : SECTION 2

2.3 A

To calculate basic earnings per share, the weighted average number of shares must be calculated as shown below.

Date	Number	Fraction of year	Weighted Average
1 January	4,000,000	3/12	1,000,000
1 April	5,000,000	9/12	3,750,000
			4,750,000

Basic EPS = $3,400,000/4,750,000 = **$0.72**

Diluted EPS calculates the interest saved, net of tax, and adds that to the earnings figure. The number of additional shares to be issued is calculated by working out the maximum shares that could be issued. In this case, the maximum number of shares that can be received is if the shareholders convert the loan into 40 shares for every $100.

To work out any interest saved the carrying amount, not the par value, should be used. The carrying amount of the liability element is $2m. Also, the effective interest rate, not the coupon rate, is used. The effective interest rate is 8%.

Additional earnings = Interest saved – additional tax.

Interest saved = $160,000 ($2m × 8%)

Additional tax = $160,000 × 26% = $41,600.

Additional earnings = (160,000 – 41,600) = $118,400

Additional shares = $2.5million × 40/100 = $1m new shares.

Diluted EPS = ($3,400,000 + $118,400)/ (4,750,000 + 1,000,000) = 61.2 cents

2.4 A

While the website is new in the year, the additional delivery costs are likely to be incurred every year in the future, meaning it is not a 'one-off' item.

2.5 A

SJ originally had control of DP. On the acquisition of the extra 20%, SJ still has control with an 80% holding. This is a control to control acquisition. The transaction is considered as a transfer between shareholders. SJ needs to treat the transaction as if cash has been paid to reduce NCI with any difference held in equity (reserves).

Therefore, to change NCI from 40% to 20% (a 20% movement in NCI), SJ has paid $937,500. NCI has reduced by 20/40 (50%) as a result.

SJ will post the following double entry:

Dr NCI	$930,000	(1,860k × 20/40 = 930k)
Dr Equity / reserves	$7,500	
Cr Cash	$937,500	

2.6 D, E

The supplier payments should be considered as revenue under IFRS 15. The payments are in return for providing advantageous shelf space and offering discounted deals on supplier products. Therefore, there are 2 performance obligations for which revenue must be recorded. This contract provides the suppliers with a service rather than transferring goods. The supplier will receive and consume benefit simultaneously, resulting in the need to recognise revenue over time.

Therefore, revenue is recognised not in advanced as per the policy of Bellamy Ltd because control is not transferred (relevant for revenue being recorded at a point in time).

When revenue is recorded over time, the stage of completion of the contract is used to determine the level of revenue recorded. As the discounted offers and the advantageous shelf space are provided over the 12months, a proportion of the total revenue should be recorded.

The Finance Director may be trying to deliberately overstate revenue by recording the payments in advance. The Finance Director (FD) could be trying to hit bonus targets and misstate the financial statements. Even if the FD was unaware of the stipulations of IFRS 15 for this payment, a person in this important role should investigate the opinions of the Financial Controller to determine the appropriate course of action. The FD does not investigate and sticks with the status quo. This is unethical. The Financial Controller would be in his rights to contact the CIMA ethics helpline.

Revenue recognition on a risk and reward basis occurs on the sale of goods. No goods are transferred in this arrangement so option C is not applicable.

The Financial Controller (FC) will follow the orders of the FD unless those orders are in direct conflict with the regulatory environment that the professional operates in. The FC will be applying IAS's in their day to day role and should comply with the ethical guidelines of their chosen profession. Accountants have strict ethical guidelines to comply with. The FC would not be following that guidance if they followed orders that they deemed to be unethical.

2.7 B

Operating margin = Profit from operations/revenue = $120,000/975,000 = **12.3%**

Revenue	975,000
Cost of sales	(555,000)
Gross profit	420,000
Operating expenses	(300,000)
Operating profit	120,000

Dividends received are held under investment income which would be below operating profit.

Dividends paid are accounted for within retained earnings and not the profit or loss account. The do not impact operating profits.

Finance costs and interest received (within investment income) are below operating profits within the profit or loss account.

ANSWERS TO OBJECTIVE TEST QUESTIONS : SECTION 2

As a result, dividends received, dividends paid and finance costs are irrelevant for the calculation of operating profit margins.

2.8 B

Growth rate is given via g = r × b

r = return = 8%

b = proportion of profits retained = (1.8 – 0.6)/1.8 = 66.7%

g = 8% × 66.7% = 5.3%

2.9 650,000 PROFIT

Sales proceeds		1,600,000
FV of retained interest		1,450,000
Less CV of sub at disposal:		
Net assets at disposal (200,000 +3,000,000)	3,200,000	
GW (fully impaired)	0	
NCI at disposal **(W)**	(800,000)	
		(2,400,000)
Profit on disposal		**650,000**

(W) Non-controlling interest at disposal

NCI at acquisition	567,500
(25% × 200,000 + 2,070,000)	
NCI% × post acquisition movement in NA's	232,500
(25% × (3,000,000 – 2,070,000))	
NCI at disposal	800,000

2.10 G

The cash flow related to NCI that should be shown in the consolidated statement of cash flows for the year ended 31 December 20X8 is:

Non-controlling interests			
Removed on disposal of the subsidiary	64,500	Brought forward	525,000
Dividends paid to NCI shareholders β	**58,500**	Total comprehensive income	201,000
Carried forward	603,000		
	726,000		726,000

Dividends paid to NCI are treated as financing activity cash flows. Dividends paid are outflows.

141

SUBJECT F2 : ADVANCED FINANCIAL REPORTING

RANDOM QUESTION TEST 3

3.1 More, higher, shorter

H is **more** liquid than C due to **higher** levels of current assets compared to current liabilities. C's liquidity could be improved if C could make its receivable days **shorter**.

Explanation:

H's current and quick ratios are higher than C's which indicates that H is more liquid than C and has greater current assets.

C's receivable days are higher than H's. If C received cash from customers earlier liquidity would improve and receivable days would be shorter.

3.2 D

The higher of the:

(i)   cash paid at redemption
(ii)   the share price converted at redemption date

is used to work out the "cash flow" on redemption in an IRR calculation for a convertible bond.

Cash option = 100 x 1.1 = $110.00

Shares option = 12 x ($8.50 x 1.04^3) = $114.74

Assume that investor will always choose the higher value option so $114.74 is the cash flow on redemption.

3.3 D

Annual foreign currency translation gain or loss can be calculated by:

		$
Closing NA's at closing rate (CR)	3,000,000/20	150,000
less		
Opening NA's @ opening rate (OR)	(3,000,000-812,500)= 2,187,500/25	(87,500)
Comprehensive income at average rate (AR)	812,500/22	(36,932)
Forex gain on translation of NA's		**25,568**

3.4 C

Liabilities are valued at their fair value. The fair value for a financial liability is the net proceeds (the nominal value less any issue costs).

The finance cost in the profit or loss account is based on the effective interest rate.

Therefore the initial liability is $45,000-$750 = $44,250.

Based on the effective interest rate, the finance charge in the statement of profit or loss will be $44,250 x 8.5% = $3,761.

ANSWERS TO OBJECTIVE TEST QUESTIONS : SECTION 2

3.5 B

Moose has entered into a lease. It should record a right-of-use asset and a lease liability. The lease liability is recorded at the present value of minimum lease payments ($87,000).

Interest will increase the liability at the rate implicit with the lease of 4.8%. Lease payments will reduce the liability.

	b/f	Finance cost at implicit rate associated with lease (4.8%)	Lease rental	c/f
20X6	87,000	4,176	(20,000)	71,176
20X7	71,176	3,416	(20,000)	54,592

The current liability at year end 20X6 will be the total liability at 31st December 20X6 ($71,176) less the total liability after the rental payments in the next year, 20X7 ($54,592).

Current liability = 71,176 – 54,592 = $16,584.

3.6 C

The dividends to include in the consolidated statement of changes in equity are:

	$
100% of LI's (P) dividend paid	1,800,000
Non-controlling interests share of VE's (Subs) dividend paid (20% × 720,000)	144,000
	1,944,000

RP is an associate. Dividends paid by an associate are not separately included within the group CSOCIE. The parent's (LI) share of the dividend paid by RP is cancelled out of the group profit or loss and, instead, the parent's share of the associates profit after tax (which includes the dividend received from the associate) is included upon equity accounting of the associate. This affects the parent's share of total comprehensive income and not the dividend paid within the CSOCIE.

3.7 D

Inventory days give the average time it takes to sell inventory. If inventory selling prices are reduced, it would be reasonably expected that the time it took to sell inventory would decrease. It would be expected that more sales of the inventory lines would occur.

Inventory obsolescence and a slowdown in trading suggest that the entity would struggle to sell the inventory lines. Thus inventory days would increase.

A change in supplier could cause changes to **payable** days as credit terms may change. However, inventory days would not be expected to be directly impacted.

SUBJECT F2 : ADVANCED FINANCIAL REPORTING

3.8 B, D

Key management personnel of a company are deemed to be related parties of the entity. The chief executive officer would meet this definition and as such is a related party.

Entities controlled by close family members of key management personnel are also deemed to be related parties. AR, the entity controlled by the chief executive officers wife is deemed a related party.

Key customers, banks and joint venturers who share joint control in a joint venture are specifically identified by IAS 24 *Related party disclosures* as NOT being related parties to an entity.

3.9 C

WACC is weighted based on market values, not nominal values.

	Market value	Cost	Weight × Cost	Weighted average
Equity	$15 million	13.2%	15/32.5 x 13.2%	6.1%
Irredeemable debt	$7.5 million	8.4%	7.5/32.5 x 8.4%	1.9%
Redeemable debt	$10 million	9.6%	10/32.5 x 9.6%	3.0%
Total	$32.5 million			11.0%

3.10 C

Goodwill in PL:	$
Consideration paid for 60% holding	5,625,000
Fair value of previous 15% holding	1,387,500
	7,012,500
Fair value of NCI at acquisition	1,800,000
Less fair value of net assets acquired	(3,750,000)
	5,062,500

ANSWERS TO OBJECTIVE TEST QUESTIONS : SECTION 2

RANDOM QUESTION TEST 4

4.1 A

Due to the extra competition within the market sector, it would be a reasonable strategy for SH to combat the competition by reducing their sales prices. If SH did lower their sales prices gross profit margin would be expected to reduce.

An increase in cost prices would cause gross profit margins to decrease. However, there are no indications within the scenario that suggest that cost prices would increase.

On this basis, whilst A & C would both contribute to gross profit margin reductions, a decrease in sales price is the most likely contributing factor. Option C is not as valid as option A.

Gross profit margin gives the % gross profit per sale. Gross profit is affected by changes in sales prices, cost prices, inefficiencies and changes in sales mix. Gross profit margins are never impacted simply through changes in volumes of sales or purchases. For volumes to impact gross profit margins, discounts on price would have to be offered in conjunction with the increase in sales volumes. Therefore, reductions in sales volumes only will not reduce GP%. Also, it can be noted that SH's sales have gone up. Option B would not be a valid conclusion.

Finance costs are included below operating profits. Gross profit margins only consider gross profits. Finance costs do not impact gross profit. Option D is not valid.

4.2 C

Despite facing more competition, SH's revenue has still increased. An increase in revenue would reasonably be expected to cause reductions in the inventory holding period (the time it takes to sell inventory on average).

The time it takes to sell inventory should not impact directly on the time it takes to repay the suppliers of SH. It could be argued that a reduction in the time it takes to sell inventory will lead to quicker eventual receipt of the cash from the customers. This could enable payables to be paid off quicker. This would cause a decrease in the payable payment period, not an increase. Option A is incorrect.

Quick ratio is calculated as current assets – inventory/current liabilities. Inventory is not included within the calculation. Quick ratio is unaffected by inventory movements. Option B is incorrect.

A decrease in inventory holding period would be expected to cause a reduction in closing stock. Reductions in closing stock would see an increase in cost of sales. As such, option D is incorrect.

4.3 B

If SH's market share has been reduced by the new product on the market, yet SH's revenue has still increased in comparison to last year, this would suggest that the overall sporting technology market is in growth.

Option A is incorrect as it appears SH has reduced their operating costs. This is indicated by the gross profit margin reducing during the year yet the operating profit margin has increased. Increased marketing expenditure would be expected to reduce the operating margin during the year. It is possible that the marketing spend did increase but operating costs savings occurred elsewhere, however there is not enough information given to make that conclusion.

Option C cannot be concluded from the information given. An increase in payment terms from suppliers may have caused the increase in SH's payable days. However, the payables increase could also be caused by the lack of cash to pay suppliers. This is evident due to the use of an overdraft during the period. It cannot be concluded that an increase in supplier credit terms caused the increase.

Option D is not a valid conclusion. SH is using an overdraft which can be an indicator of some liquidity issues. There is no evidence to suggest that the overdraft usage is in breach of SH's authorised limits. As such, it cannot be concluded that SH is insolvent.

4.4 **C**

NB. This question requires the cum div share price. That is the share price **before** the dividend payment.

ke with dividend growth =

$$k_e = \frac{d_0 \times (1+g)}{P_0} + g$$

$$P_0 = \frac{d_0 \times (1+g)}{k_e - g}$$

$$P_0 = \frac{0.5 \times 1.07}{0.149 - 0.07} = 6.77$$

Ex div price = 6.77

Cum div price = 6.77 + 0.5

Cum div price = 7.27

4.5 **A**

The transaction is treated as if GP received cash to increase NCI. Any difference is posted to equity.

The correct DE is:

Dr Equity 99,000

Dr Cash 385,000

Cr NCI 484,000 (W)

(W) The movement in NCI is calculated as:

	$,000
MD's NA's at disposal	2,200
MD's goodwill at disposal	220
	2,420
NCI movement (20% - 40%)	20%
	484

ANSWERS TO OBJECTIVE TEST QUESTIONS : SECTION 2

4.6 D

CD has made an investment in bonds that would be treated as a financial asset.

The asset would be classified and measured at amortised cost. The bonds are debt financial assets and CD has the intention to hold them until the maturity date. This is consistent with CD's overall business model for similar financial assets.

The transaction costs of $12,800 (0.5% x $2,560,000) would be added to the asset at initial recognition. (NB. Both the $2,560,000 and $12,800 are outflows of cash).

The transaction costs would only be treated as an expense if the asset was classified as FVPL.

4.7 2,106,667

SARs are valued at:
- FV of the SAR at the year-end
- Multiplied by the number of SAR's expected to vest
- Spread over the vesting period.

Y/e 20X1

6 x 2000 × (360-20-40)/3 =1,200,000

Dr P/L 1,200,000 Cr Liability 1,200,000

Y/e 20X2

8 × 2000 × (360 -20-20-10) × 2/3 = $3,306,667

(less previously recognised expense from 20X1) – 1,200,000 = $2,106,667

Dr P/L 2,106,667 Cr Liability 2,106,667

4.8 B

The cost of investment is included at the fair value of consideration.

The fair value of shares issued as consideration is the market value at the acquisition date. The market value of HI's shares issued at 30th June 20X4 was $3.80.

Shares in HI: 800,000 × ¾ × $3.80 = $2,280,000

The fair value of deferred cash is the present value of the payments.

Deferred cash = $550,000 × 1/1.1 = $500,000

The professional fees cannot be capitalised as part of the cost of investment. Therefore the total fair value of the consideration is $2,280,000 + $500,000 = **$2,780,000**

4.9 B, D

The share price is only one way of measuring a company's value. Its market capitalisation (share price multiplied by number of shares) is widely used by investment analysts but there is no "exact" measure of a company's value.

A stock market flotation is expensive and time consuming due to, for example, advisor fees and legal fees.

The original owners must dilute their shareholding by making shares available for the public to buy on the flotation.

4.10 D

Option A is incorrect. It is accurate so far as to say that impairment is not a cash flow – it is an expense. However, the impairment expense will cause an adjustment to the reconciliation from profit before tax to cash generated from operations. The impairment does effect the cash flow statement.

Option B is incorrect. The NET cash outflow from acquiring a subsidiary is included in "cash flows from investing activities" not the GROSS cash flow. The net cash flow includes the gross amount paid to acquire the subsidiary less the cash held by the sub at acquisition (that is 100% consolidated as part of the CSOFP).

Option C is incorrect. The dividend received from the associates is an actual cash inflow for the group and is included within "cash flows from investing activities". The parent's share of associate's profits will be adjusted as part of the reconciliation to calculate "cash generated from operations", not the dividend received.

RANDOM QUESTION TEST 5

5.1 A

DA directly controls VI with a 75% shareholding. The NCI holding in VI is 25%. VI directly controls BO with a 60% shareholding.

BO is an indirectly controlled sub-subsidiary of DA. BO would be consolidated using the effective shareholding of 75% × 65% = 45%. NCI of the sub-sub is 55%.

On the calculation of goodwill for BO, an indirect holding adjustment is required that adjusts for the Sub's (VI) NCI's contribution to the purchase of the sub-sub. The indirect holding adjustment is given as the Sub's NCI × cost of investment in BO.

The indirect holding adjustment is calculated as 25% × 8,000,000 = $2,000,000.

5.2 A, C

The date a sub-sub is consolidated is the date of effective control. This is the later of the date the parent buys the sub or the date the sub buys the sub-sub.

In the case of DA's sub-sub, BO, the later date is the date the parent buys the sub-sub. DA purchases its sub, VI, on the 31st January 20X8. VI purchased BO in 20X6. BO is not part of the DA group at this point. BO only becomes part of the group once DA buys VI in 20X8. Both the sub and the sub-sub have the same acquisition date for the DA group.

A shareholding of over 50% of an entity's ordinary share capital is typically enough for control to be achieved. DA owns 75% of VI. This is enough for control to be achieved. VI would be deemed to be a subsidiary of DA.

Option B is incorrect. BO is an indirectly controlled sub-subsidiary of DA. BO would be consolidated using the effective shareholding of 75% × 65% = 45%. Therefore, the NCI of BO is 55%, not 45%.

Option D is incorrect. DA has indirect control over BO, not significant influence. BO is consolidated as a sub-subsidiary to reflect the control. Equity accounting is used only for associates and joint ventures.

Option E is incorrect. Impairment charges will be split between parent and NCI's only if the parent uses the fair value method to calculate NCI and goodwill. As DA uses the proportionate method for VI's goodwill, any future impairment will not be allocated to NCI's. The entire impairment would be allocated to DA's profits and retained earnings only.

Only the impairment on BO would be allocated to NCI as the fair value method is in use.

ANSWERS TO OBJECTIVE TEST QUESTIONS : SECTION 2

5.3 **B**

Goodwill of BO as at 31st Jan 20X9

	$000
Consideration paid	8,000
Indirect holding adjustment (25% × 8,000,000)	(2,000)
DA share of consideration paid	6,000
Fair value of non-controlling interest at acquisition (20X8)	1,650
Less fair value of net assets at acquisition (W)	(6,650)
Goodwill at acquisition	1,000
Less impairment	0
Goodwill at the reporting date	1,000

(W) Net assets of BO as at acquisition 31st Jan 20X8

	$000
Share capital	2,000
Retained earnings	4,200
Fair value adjustment – non-depreciable land	450
	6,650

5.4 **D**

The group retained earnings will include DA's % of the post-acquisition profits of VI. This is given as 75% of $1,600,000 (W) = 1,200,000.

(W) Post acquisition profits = retained earnings at reporting date − retained earnings as at acquisition date = 5,250,000 − 3,650,000 = $1,600,000.

No extra depreciation of the fair value adjustment is required. The fair value adjustment relates to non-depreciable land.

5.5 **D**

A lease will initially record the lease liability and the right-of-use asset. The lease liability is recorded at the present value of remaining lease payments. The right-of-use asset is recorded at the lease liability plus initial direct costs ($2.000) plus payments already made (deposit of 5,000).

The right of use asset is recorded on 1 July 20X7 as 29,844 (W1) + 2,000 + 5,000 = $36,844

(W1) The present value of remaining lease payments discounted at 10% = $12,000 × 2.487 = $29,844

This is depreciated over the lower of the lease term or the economic lifetime of 3 years.

Only 6 months of depreciation would be charged to the right-of-use asset during the year ended 31 December 20X7.

SUBJECT F2 : ADVANCED FINANCIAL REPORTING

The carrying amount at 31 December 20X7 is:

Initial right-of-use asset	36,844
Depreciation 36,844/3 × 6/12	(6,141)
	30,703

5.6 B

Published financial statements should not contain material errors, as, for most companies, they have been audited. Non-material errors will be contained within the financial statements but should not be of a magnitude that will impact the trends of ratio analysis. Errors are not a limitation of ratio analysis; they are a problem with the preparation of financial statements.

5.7 B

Earnings per share

EPS = $4,200,000/4,713,333 (W1) = 89.1c

(W1) Weighted average number of shares

Step 1 – Theoretical ex-rights price (TERP)

2 shares @ $2 =	$4
1 share @ $1.40 =	$1.40
3 shares	$5.40

TERP = $5.40/3 = $1.80

Step 2 – Rights issue bonus fraction

Cum rights price	2.00
Theoretical ex rights price	1.80

Step 3 – Weighted average number of shares

Date	Number	Fraction of year	Rights fraction	Weighted Average
1 January	3,360,000	3/12	2/1.8	933,333
1 April	5,040,000	9/12		3,780,000
				4,713,333

5.8 9.61%

Year	Cash flow	Discount factor at 5%	Present value	Discount factor at 10%	Present value
0	-98	1.000	-98	1.000	-98
1-3	5	2.723	13.62	2.487	12.44
3	112.5	0.864	97.20	0.751	84.49
			12.82		-1.07

YTM = 5% + [(10%-5%) × 12.82/(12.82 + 1.07)] = 9.61%

ANSWERS TO OBJECTIVE TEST QUESTIONS : SECTION 2

5.9 C

As per IFRS 2 *Share based payments*, equity-settled share-based payments are valued at:
- fair value at the grant date
- based upon expected number of options to vest
- spread over vesting period

Expense for y/e 31 December 20X1

	$
(400 – 24 – 56) × 500 × FV$1.60	256,000
Spread over vesting period	/3
	85,333

Expense for y/e 31 December 20X2

	$
(400-24-26-24) × 500 × 1.60 = spread over vesting 2/3	260,800
	173,867
Less previously recognised	(85,333)
	88,534

5.10 B, C

Investments in post-employment benefits plans like defined benefit pension schemes and investments that fall under the remit of IFRS 9 *Financial instruments* are specifically mentioned as being outside the scope of IFRS 12 *Disclosure of Interests in Other Entities*.

SUBJECT F2 : ADVANCED FINANCIAL REPORTING

Section 3

REFERENCES

The Board (2016) *Conceptual Framework for Financial Reporting*. London: IFRS Foundation.

The Board (2016) *IAS 7 Statement of Cash Flows*. London: IFRS Foundation.

The Board (2016) *IAS 12 Income Taxes*. London: IFRS Foundation.

The Board (2016) *IAS 17 Leases*. London: IFRS Foundation.

The Board (2016) *IAS 21 The Effects of Changes in Foreign Exchange Rates*. London: IFRS Foundation.

The Board (2016) *IAS 24 Related Party Disclosures*. London: IFRS Foundation.

The Board (2016) *IAS 27 Separate Financial Statements*. London: IFRS Foundation.

The Board (2016) *IAS 28 Investments in Associates and Joint Ventures*. London: IFRS Foundation.

The Board (2016) *IAS 32 Financial Instruments: Presentation*. London: IFRS Foundation.

The Board (2016) *IAS 33 Earnings per Share*. London: IFRS Foundation.

The Board (2016) *IAS 36 Impairment of Assets*. London: IFRS Foundation.

The Board (2016) *IAS 37 Provisions, Contingent Liabilities and Contingent Assets*. London: IFRS Foundation.

The Board (2016) *IAS 38 Intangible Assets*. London: IFRS Foundation.

The Board (2016) *IAS 39 Financial Instruments: Recognition and measurement*. London: IFRS Foundation.

The Board (2016) *IFRS 2 Share-based Payment*. London: IFRS Foundation.

The Board (2016) *IFRS 3 Business Combinations*. London: IFRS Foundation.

The Board (2016) *IFRS 7 Financial Instruments: Disclosure*. London: IFRS Foundation.

The Board (2016) *IFRS 8 Operating Segments*. London: IFRS Foundation.

The Board (2016) *IFRS 9 Financial Instruments*. London: IFRS Foundation.

The Board (2016) *IFRS 10 Consolidated Financial Statements*. London: IFRS Foundation.

The Board (2016) *IFRS 11 Joint Arrangements*. London: IFRS Foundation.

The Board (2016) *IFRS 12 Disclosure of Interests in Other Entities*. London: IFRS Foundation.

The Board (2016) *IFRS 13 Fair Value Measurement*. London: IFRS Foundation.

The Board (2016) *IFRS 15 Revenue from contracts with customers*. London: IFRS Foundation.

The Board (2016) *IFRS 16 Leases*. London: IFRS Foundation.